Thinking skills

A cross-curricular approach

Remembering

Understanding

Applying

Analysing

Evaluating

Creating

6402C

54 / 5

THINKING SKILLS *(Middle)*

Published by Prim-Ed Publishing 2006
Copyright© R.I.C. Publications® 2006
ISBN 978-1-84654-075-2
PR–6402

Additional titles available in this series:
THINKING SKILLS *(Lower)*
THINKING SKILLS *(Upper)*

Internet websites

In some cases, websites or specific URLs may be recommended. While these are checked and rechecked at the time of publication, the publisher has no control over any subsequent changes which may be made to webpages. It is *strongly* recommended that the class teacher checks *all* URLs before allowing pupils to access them.

View all pages online

Website: www.prim-ed.com

Email: sales@prim-ed.com

Foreword

Thinking skills is a series of three books, designed to provide opportunities for pupils to practise the six thinking skills of *Bloom's revised taxonomy*—remembering, understanding, applying, analysing, evaluating and creating—across the learning areas of English, Maths, Science, History/Geography, PE/Health/Values and The Arts. The skills are ranked in order from the three, fundamental, lower order skills to the three more advanced, higher order skills.

Titles in this series are:

Thinking skills (Lower)
Thinking skills (Middle)
Thinking skills (Upper)

Contents

Teachers notes

The purpose of this book is to provide a practical resource of learning activities, each aimed at a specific thinking skill as described in *Bloom's revised taxonomy*. Pupils require these skills to understand and process a vast amount of information from a range of media and to consider its relevance and validity. The range of tasks provided will encourage and assist pupils to become higher level thinkers.

A brief explanation of *Bloom's revised taxonomy*

In the 1950s, Benjamin Bloom developed the *Taxonomy of Educational Objectives* as a means of expressing, qualitatively, different kinds of thinking. It continues to be one of the most widely applied models of formal analysis of the nature of thinking and has been adapted for use in school curriculum planning.

Bloom's original taxonomy provided a means of organising thinking skills into six levels ranging from the most basic to the more complex. These terms were revised in the 1990s by Lorin Anderson, a former pupil of Bloom, resulting in some significant improvements to the existing model.

Bloom's original terms	Anderson's revised terms
Knowledge	Remembering
Comprehension	Understanding
Application	Applying
Analysis	Analysing
Synthesis	Evaluating
Evaluation	Creating

The names of the six major categories were changed to verb forms as thinking is an active process. Remembering replaced knowledge as the first level of thinking as knowledge is an outcome rather than a type of thinking. In keeping with the nature of thinking described for each level, comprehension and evaluation were renamed understanding and creating, respectively. Where Bloom's original taxonomy was aimed at the early years of schooling, Anderson's revised taxonomy is more universal and applicable at all levels of study.

The six levels of thinking are ranked from the three lower order skills of remembering, understanding and applying to the higher order skills of analysing, evaluating and creating.

At each level of the taxonomy, there are subcategories which describe the emphasis of each skill.

Skill	Subcategories
remembering	recognising, recalling, listing, describing, identifying, retrieving, locating, naming, finding
understanding	interpreting, exemplifying, classifying, summarising, inferring, comparing, explaining
applying	executing, implementing, using, carrying out
analysing	differentiating, organising, attributing, comparing, deconstructing, outlining, structuring
evaluating	checking, hypothesising, experimenting, judging, testing, detecting, monitoring
creating	generating, planning, producing, designing, constructing, inventing, devising, making

Why teach thinking skills?

It is widely acknowledged that if pupils are to become better thinkers, they must be taught explicitly how to think. Planning for this explicit teaching is essential. Teaching methods must promote the transfer of learning beyond one context and into others. To develop better thinking skills, pupils require an environment which demonstrates an open-minded attitude to the nature of knowledge and thinking, providing open-ended tasks with multiple solutions. Talking about thinking, using all strategies for questioning, should be actively encouraged and form a part of all learning situations.

Focusing on thinking skills supports active cognitive processing, helping pupils to investigate beyond the information provided and to assess each situation before reaching their own conclusions.

Teachers notes

Questioning

A key element in the development of thinking skills is questioning. To engage pupils in thought at each level, questions need to be used purposefully, directing pupils to achieve defined goals. Open-ended questioning allows pupils to demonstrate their ability in each thinking skill.

Questions at the lower levels of the taxonomy encourage …	Questions at the higher levels of the taxonomy encourage …
recalling information	*determining different parts of any object, text or concept and exploring them*
explaining ideas or concepts	*justifying opinions, decisions and courses of action*
using knowledge in different situations	*developing new ideas or models based on previous knowledge*

Each pupil activity page includes a number of questions, relevant to the activity, for the pupils to consider. By reflecting on each, they will have the opportunity to develop their metacognitive thought processes.

Metacognition

In order to improve each thinking skill and to establish meaning from information, pupils need to develop their own thought processes. Metacognitive thought enables an individual to recognise preferred learning strategies and to consciously direct his/her learning.

Metacognition, which means to 'think about thinking', was first described as a learning concept in 1976 by John Flavell. It comprises three parts:

- *Metamemory* – an awareness of different memory strategies, a knowledge of which strategy is best suited for a task and how it may be used most effectively.

  Pupils develop a plan for learning which occurs before learning.

- *Metacomprehension* – the ability to check understanding of information, to identify gaps in understanding and to rectify identified failures.

  Pupils monitor and adjust the plan which occurs during learning.

- *Self-regulation* – the ability to modify learning processes in response to perceived feedback.

  Pupils evaluate the plan after the learning process has taken place.

There are a number of recognised analyses of the nature of thinking, all aiming to develop thinking to a qualitatively higher level; for example:

Six thinking hats – *Edward de Bono*

Instrumental enrichment – *Reuven Feuerstein*

Philosophy for children – *Matthew Lipman*

Multiple intelligences – *Howard Gardner*

Thinkers keys – *Tony Ryan*

Cognitive and cooperative thinking strategies – *Eric Frangenheim*

Cooperative learning structures which develop thinking skills – *Spencer Kagan*.

Teachers notes

Graphic organisers

What is a graphic organiser?

A graphic organiser is a means of presenting information pictorially. Blank areas are provided for pupils to record ideas or information about a given topic.

There are a number of graphic organiser styles, each of which is suited for a particular purpose. The basic design of any organiser may be adapted to meet the requirements of a specific task and level of ability.

Purpose	Examples
concept development	concept map, spider map, word map, character map, mind map, story map, story star, concept web, summary chart, matrix, T-chart, Y-chart, 5W chart, KWL chart, senses chart, step chart, comparison/contrast chart, paragraph organiser frame, structured overview, note making framework, issues circle, futures wheel
presenting data	bar chart, pictogram, line graph, pie chart, labelled diagram, array
determining sequences	word chain, sequence chain, word wheel, cycle wheel, ladder, historical time line, continuum, flow chart, cartoon and picture strip, action plan, rebus
evaluating	PMI chart, plus/minus T-chart, agreement scales, evaluation scales (plus, minus, interesting)
determining relationships	fishbone map, concentric circle chart, semantic grid, decision tree, network tree, human interaction outline
categorising and classifying	plot, matrix, pyramid, categories, Venn diagram, Carroll diagram, arrow diagram, tree diagram

Why use graphic organisers?

- Graphic organisers show the key facts, ideas or results of a given situation or topic.
- They help to clarify thoughts and to determine how to proceed.
- The information illustrated is immediately obvious without the need for reading and analysing lengthy text.
- Pupils learn that presenting information in this way is an important means of communicating ideas and information.
- It demonstrates understanding of their own research and similar representations in the media worldwide.

Using a graphic organiser

To gain confidence in completing and studying graphic organisers, pupils need to be:

- presented with many tasks which require pictorial representation
- guided in their choice of style(s) and in the conventions of that style, so they can develop effective representations related to a given purpose and audience.

Teachers need to discuss and model each style of organiser as it is introduced, explaining how it works for a given purpose and how it can be adapted if required.

Teachers notes

Examples of graphic organisers:

Concept map

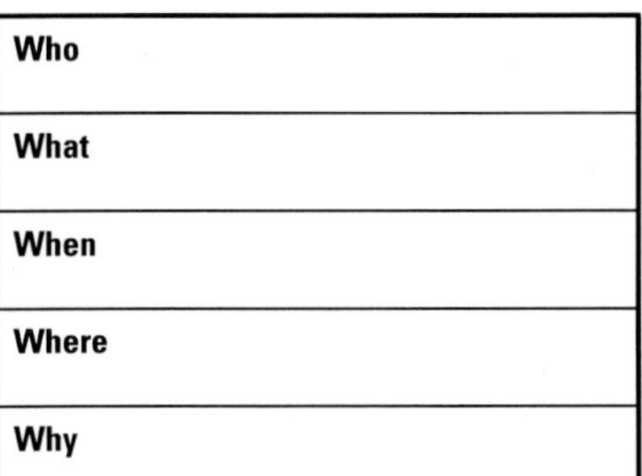

5W chart

Pie chart

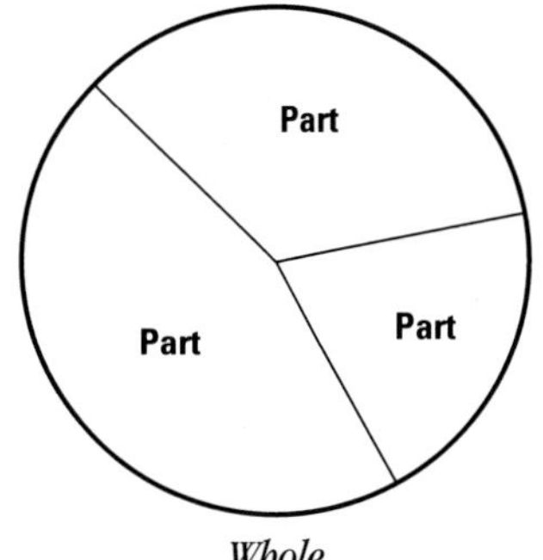

Whole

Flow chart

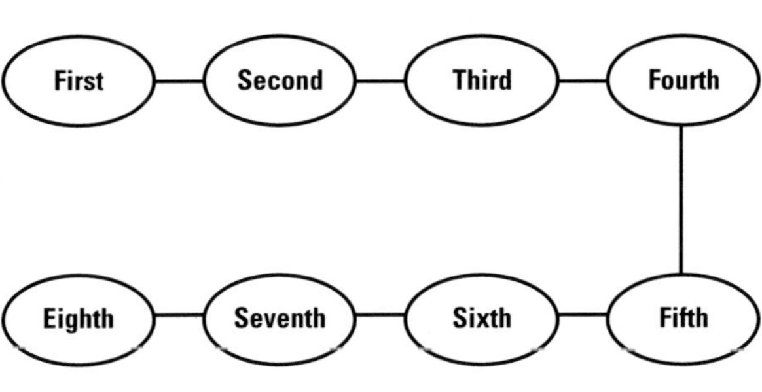

Chain

Evaluation chart

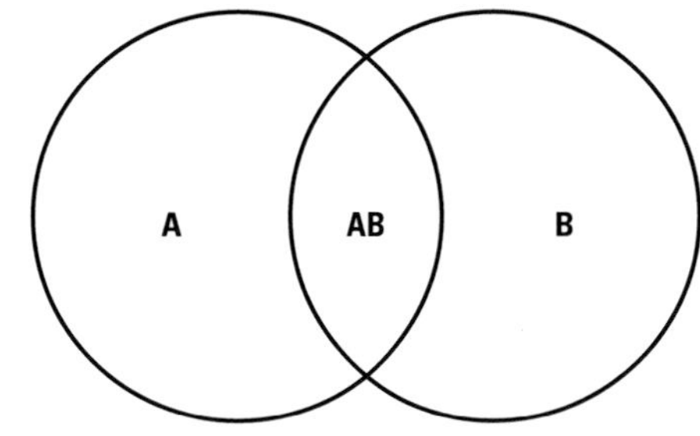

PMI chart

Fishbone chart

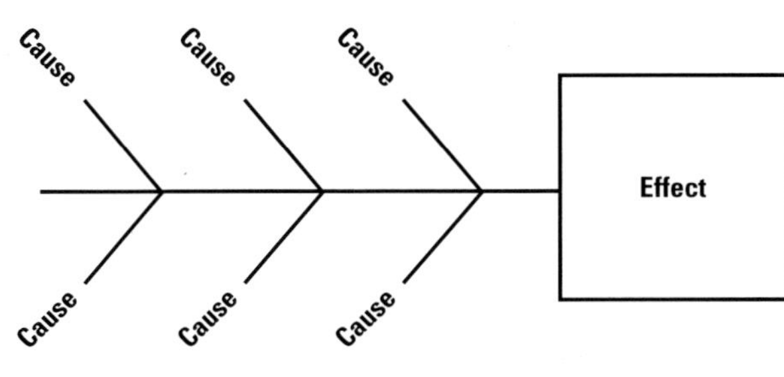

Fishbone

Compare/Contrast organisers

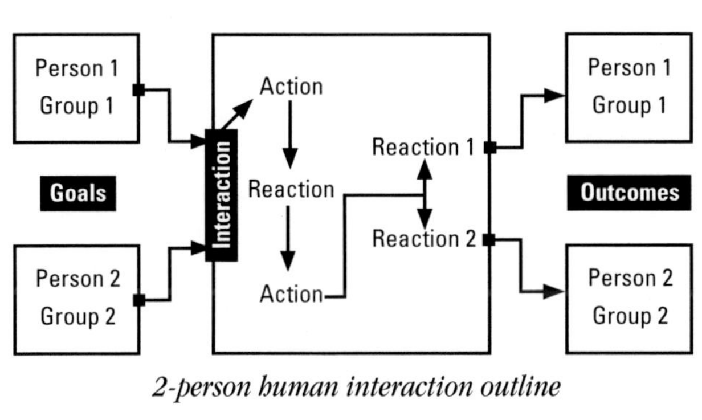

Venn diagram

Human interaction outline

2-person human interaction outline

Story star

5-point story star

Teachers notes

The six thinking skills of Bloom's revised taxonomy have been used:

• *remembering*   • *understanding*   • *applying*   • *analysing*   • *evaluating*   • *creating*

Each section has a cover page, a pupil self-evaluation page and a teacher introduction page.

For each skill, an activity from each key learning area has been provided.

• *English*   • *Mathematics*   • *The Arts*   • *Science*   • *History/Geography*
• *Physical Education/Health/Values*

Each activity is presented over two pages; a pupil page and a teachers page. At the end of each section, two theme-based, extension thinking challenges are provided. The final page of the book includes references for further research.

Pupil cover page

The pupil cover page allows pupils to collate worksheets dealing with a particular thinking skill.

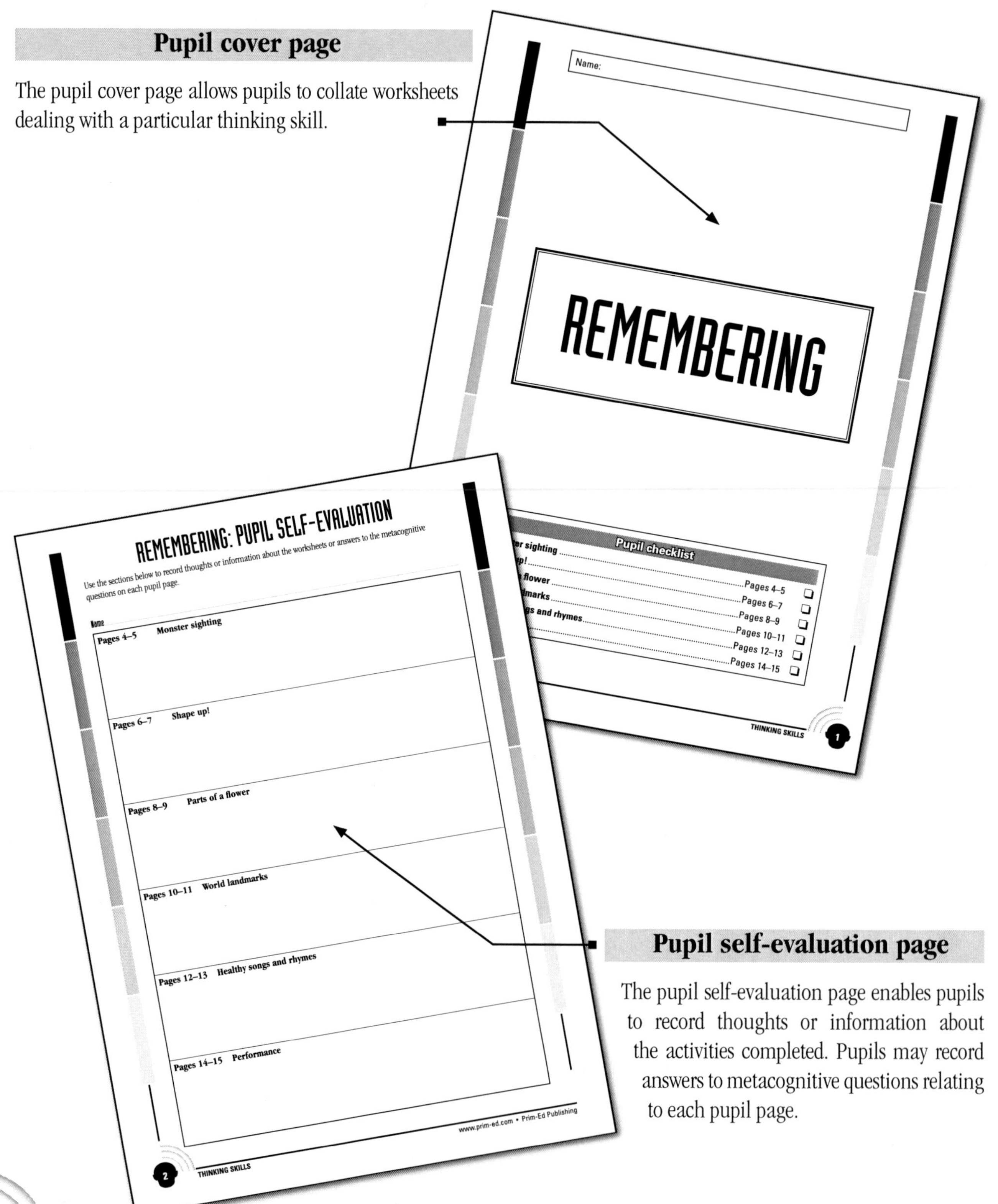

Pupil self-evaluation page

The pupil self-evaluation page enables pupils to record thoughts or information about the activities completed. Pupils may record answers to metacognitive questions relating to each pupil page.

Teachers notes

Teacher introduction page

Section summary chart, provides page numbers, title of pupil page, key learning area and task objectives.

Definition, provides full definition of thinking skill.

Appropriate verbs, offers suggestions for command verbs to use to help pupils to focus on the specific skill.

Appropriate graphic organisers, offers suggestions for graphic organisers to use to assist pupils focus their thinking within each skill.

Appropriate questions, offers suggestions for questions to ask to help pupils practise the specific skill.

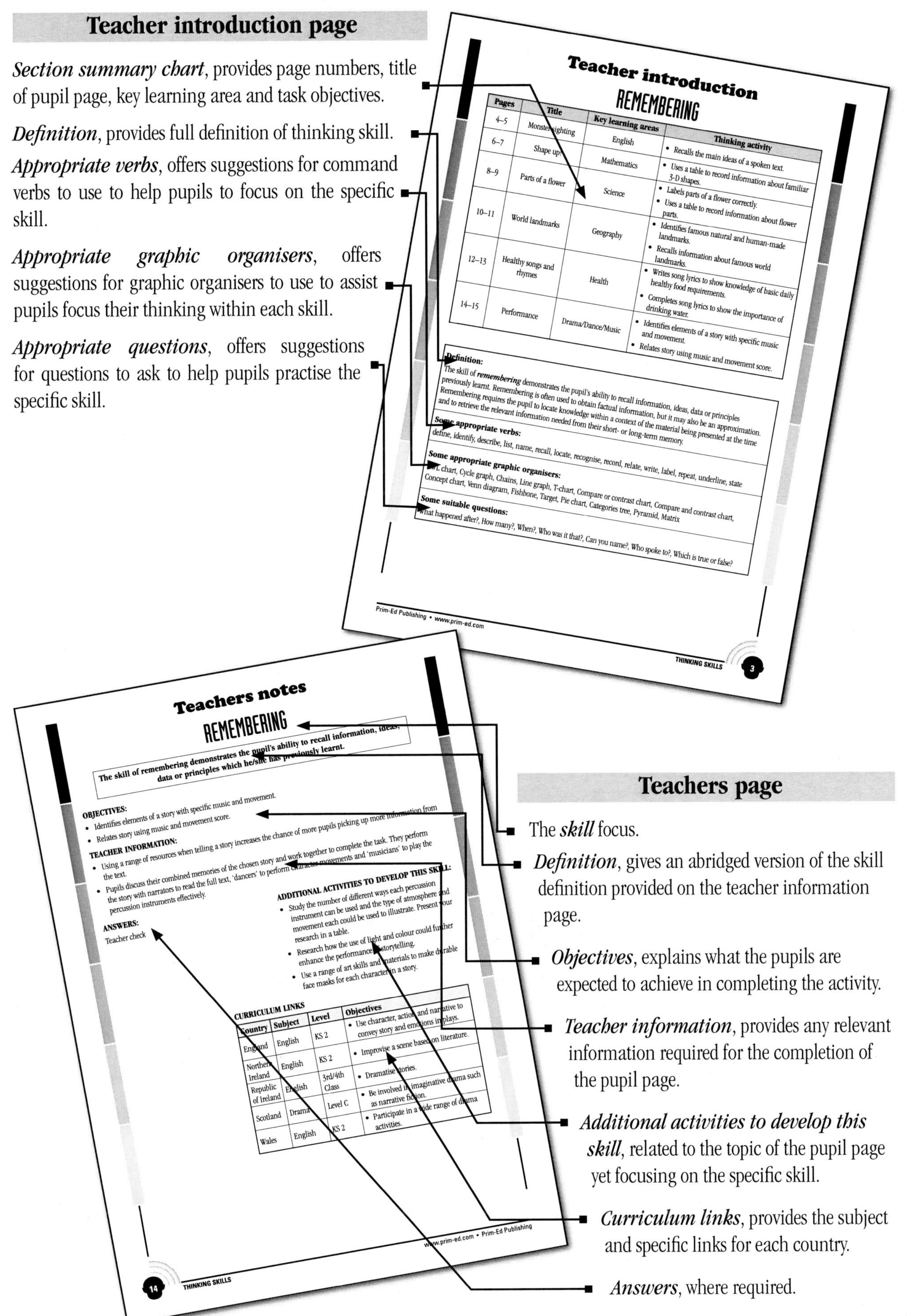

Teachers page

The *skill* focus.

Definition, gives an abridged version of the skill definition provided on the teacher information page.

Objectives, explains what the pupils are expected to achieve in completing the activity.

Teacher information, provides any relevant information required for the completion of the pupil page.

Additional activities to develop this skill, related to the topic of the pupil page yet focusing on the specific skill.

Curriculum links, provides the subject and specific links for each country.

Answers, where required.

Teachers notes

Pupil page

The *title* of the page.

The *task*, explains what the pupils will do.

The *activity*, the range of which varies throughout the book, across the six learning areas.

Thinking more about thinking, to help pupils develop their metacognitive thought processes before, during and after the activity.

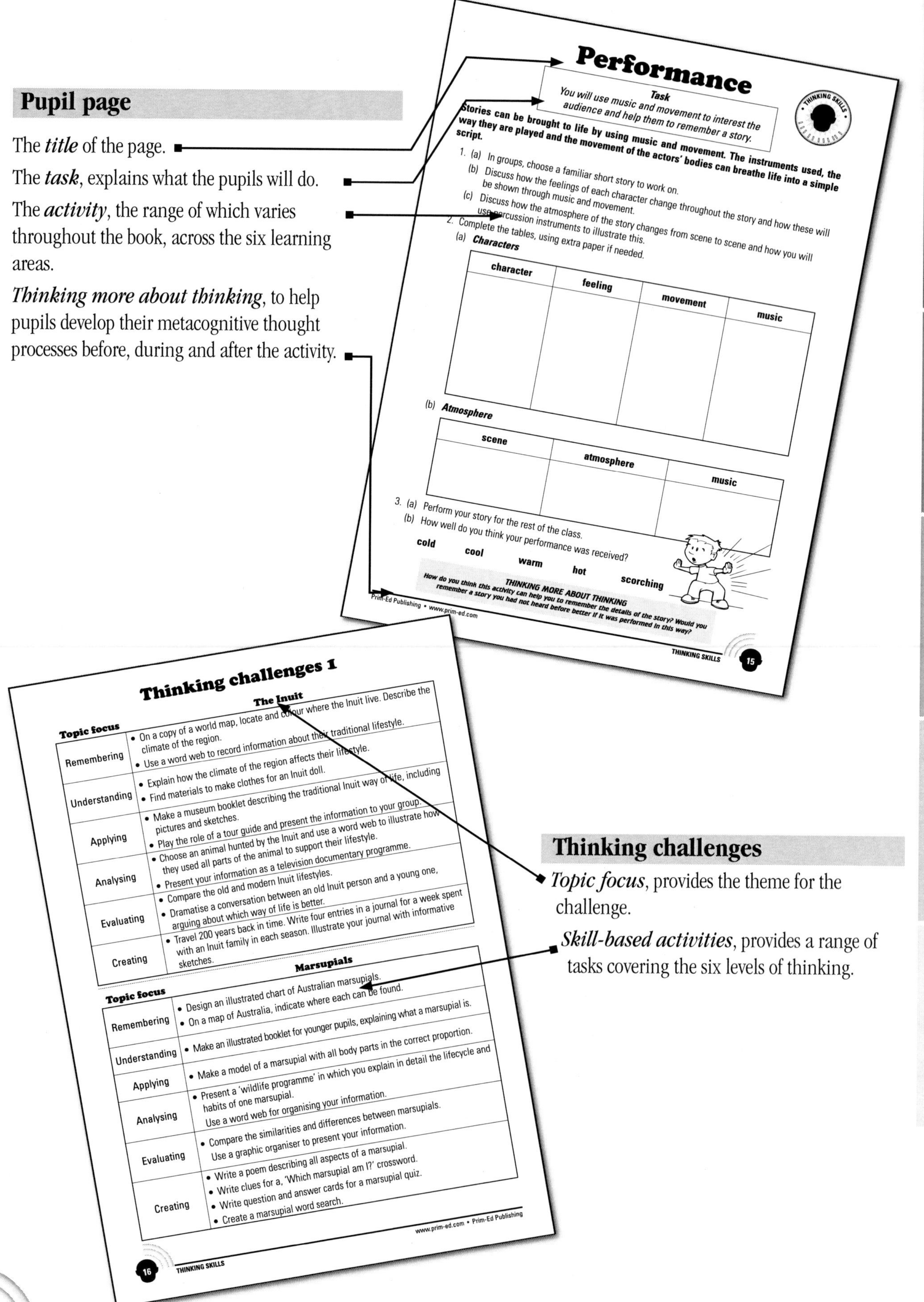

Thinking challenges

Topic focus, provides the theme for the challenge.

Skill-based activities, provides a range of tasks covering the six levels of thinking.

Name:

REMEMBERING

Use the sections below to record thoughts or information about the worksheets or answers to the metacognitive questions on each pupil page.

Name

Pages 4–5	**Monster sighting**
Pages 6–7	**Shape up!**
Pages 8–9	**Parts of a flower**
Pages 10–11	**World landmarks**
Pages 12–13	**Healthy songs and rhymes**
Pages 14–15	**Performance**

Teacher introduction
REMEMBERING

Pages	Title	Key learning areas	Thinking activity
4–5	Monster sighting	English	• Recalls the main ideas of a spoken text.
6–7	Shape up!	Mathematics	• Uses a table to record information about familiar 3-D shapes.
8–9	Parts of a flower	Science	• Labels parts of a flower correctly. • Uses a table to record information about flower parts.
10–11	World landmarks	Geography	• Identifies famous natural and human-made landmarks. • Recalls information about famous world landmarks.
12–13	Healthy songs and rhymes	Health	• Writes song lyrics to show knowledge of basic daily healthy food requirements. • Completes song lyrics to show the importance of drinking water.
14–15	Performance	Drama/Dance/Music	• Identifies elements of a story with specific music and movement. • Relates story using music and movement score.

Definition:

The skill of *remembering* demonstrates the pupil's ability to recall information, ideas, data or principles previously learnt. Remembering is often used to obtain factual information, but it may also be an approximation. Remembering requires the pupil to locate knowledge within a context of the material being presented at the time and to retrieve the relevant information needed from their short- or long-term memory.

Some appropriate verbs:

define, identify, describe, list, name, recall, locate, recognise, record, relate, write, label, repeat, underline, state

Some appropriate graphic organisers:

KWL chart, Cycle graph, Chains, Line graph, T-chart, Compare or contrast chart, Compare and contrast chart, Concept chart, Venn diagram, Fishbone, Target, Pie chart, Categories tree, Pyramid, Matrix

Some suitable questions:

What happened after?, How many?, When?, Who was it that?, Can you name?, Who spoke to?, Which is true or false?

Teachers notes

REMEMBERING

> **The skill of remembering demonstrates the pupil's ability to recall information, ideas, data or principles which he/she has previously learnt.**

OBJECTIVE:

- Recalls the main ideas of a spoken text.

TEACHER INFORMATION:

- Read the following text to the pupils slowly and clearly. After reading the text, read aloud the activities on the pupil page for the pupils. You may read the text again after this if required, but do not allow the pupils to read the text or take notes.

You work at a tourist information centre near Loch Ness in Scotland—the supposed home of the Loch Ness monster, or 'Nessie'. One day, you receive a phone call from a tourist who claims to have recently sighted the monster. You try to remember the main details of what the person says so you can pass the information on to other tourists. This is what the caller tells you:

'I was walking near the loch at sunrise a few days ago, on the 12th of March, when I saw *Nessie*. Through my binoculars, I saw her emerge slowly and gracefully from the water. She had caught a fish and was eating it. *Nessie* was huge—about three times the size of an elephant. She had a long neck like a giraffe. As I watched, she swam to the edge of the lake and lumbered clumsily out of the water. She seemed to find it difficult to move on land. She settled herself down and made a sound like a foghorn—it was surprisingly low and soft. *Nessie* then began eating the plants that grow along the loch's edge, making snuffling noises. She was dark green, with some black spots on her smooth skin and had four flippers, two humps on her back and a long, thin tail. She was definitely dinosaur-like. Unfortunately, after only a few minutes, she spotted me. This startled her and she immediately plunged back into the water and disappeared.'

ANSWERS:

Answers will vary, but should be similar to the following:

Time and date of sighting: sunrise, 12 March

Length of sighting: a few minutes

Physical appearance: three times the size of an elephant, long neck like a giraffe, dark green, black spots, smooth skin, four flippers, two humps on back, long, thin tail, dinosaur-like

Sounds: low and soft call like a foghorn, snuffling noises when eating

Diet: fish and plants

Movements: slow and graceful in water, lumbered clumsily on land – found it difficult to move

ADDITIONAL ACTIVITIES TO DEVELOP THIS SKILL:

- Read aloud a range of fiction and nonfiction texts to the pupils and then ask them to answer a set of quiz questions about each.
- After listening to radio news reports, list the main points of one of the stories.
- Have the pupils retell simple narratives they have heard, using their own words.

CURRICULUM LINKS

Country	Subject	Level	Objectives
England	English	KS 2	• Identify the gist and key points of an account and recall important features of talk.
Northern Ireland	Language and literacy	KS 2	• Listen and respond to texts and retell stories.
Republic of Ireland	English	3rd/4th Class	• Listen to and retell a description.
Scotland	English	Level C	• Produce written accounts of what they have heard.
Wales	English	KS 2	• Listen carefully, recall and re-present important features of a talk and identify the gist and key points.

THINKING SKILLS www.prim-ed.com • Prim-Ed Publishing

Monster sighting

> **Task**
> *You will listen to a description and use the information to complete a poster.*

After hanging up the phone, you use the caller's information to create a poster to place in the tourist information centre.

Recent Loch Ness monster sighting

Time and date of sighting: ______________________________

Length of sighting: ______________________________

Details:

Physical appearance:	Sounds:
	Dict:
	Movements:

Below is a labelled picture of the monster, based on the information we received.

Teachers notes
REMEMBERING

The skill of remembering demonstrates the pupil's ability to recall information, ideas, data or principles which he/she has previously learnt.

OBJECTIVE:

- Uses a table to record information about familiar 3-D shapes.

TEACHER INFORMATION:

- Recording using graphic organisers helps pupils to organise their thoughts and information into a logical format which is easy for them and others to understand. Pupils can quickly see how information is related, how content may be connected and what information might be missing.

ANSWERS:

Shape	Name of shape	Number of faces	Number of edges	Number of vertices
(a)	cube	6	12	8
(b)	cylinder	3	2	0
(c)	rectangular prism/cuboid	6	12	8
(d)	sphere	1	0	0
(e)	triangular pyramid	4	6	4
(f)	cone	2	1	1

ADDITIONAL ACTIVITIES TO DEVELOP THIS SKILL:

- Choose two 3-D shapes and construct a comparison chart which shows the similarities and differences between them.
- Describe a 3-D shape for a classmate to guess the name of the shape.
- Write a description of a particular 3-D shape to match an illustration using correct mathematical terminology such as edges, vertices and faces.
- Draw a 3-D shape to match a given description.
- Name the 2-D shapes which match particular 3-D shapes; for example, square and cube.
- Write a definition for each 3-D shape; for example, 'A sphere is . . .'.
- Complete questions about 3-D shapes such as 'Which two 3-D shapes have 6 faces, 12 edges and 8 vertices?' (cube and rectangular prism), 'Which two 3-D shapes have no vertices?' (cylinder and sphere) etc.

CURRICULUM LINKS

Country	Subject	Level	Objectives
England	Maths	KS 2	• Recognise the geometrical features and properties of 3-D shapes.
Northern Ireland	Maths and numeracy	KS 2	• Investigate the number of faces, edges and vertices on 3-D shapes.
Republic of Ireland	Maths	3rd/4th Class	• Explore and describe the properties of 3-D shapes; e.g. number of faces, edges and corners.
Scotland	Maths	Level D	• Discuss 3-D shapes, referring to faces, edges and vertices.
Wales	Maths	KS 2	• Recognise the geometrical features and properties of 3-D shapes.

Shape up!

> **Task**
> You will identify and record information about familiar 3-D shapes.

Complete the table for each shape.

Shape	Name of shape	Number of faces	Number of edges	Number of vertices
(a) 				
(b)				
(c)				
(d)				
(e)				
(f)				

THINKING MORE ABOUT THINKING
What clues, if any, do you use to remember the names of different 3-D shapes? Do you find that you remember some things easily because you are a visual/spatial learner?

Teachers notes
REMEMBERING

The skill of remembering demonstrates the pupil's ability to recall information, ideas, data or principles which he/she has previously learnt.

OBJECTIVES:

- Labels parts of a flower correctly.
- Uses a table to record information about flower parts.

TEACHER INFORMATION:

- Using a table to record information helps to clarify concepts for the pupils. Although they can easily name some parts of a flower, they are not always so familiar with the reproductive parts. When they are clear about what the parts are, they will be more able to understand the role of each part in the reproduction process.
- The **petals** of a flower attract pollinators (insects) into the flower.
- The **male** reproductive organs of a flower are called the stamen (anther and filament). The pollen consists of **male** reproductive cells.
- The **anthers** contain the pollen sacs. The pollen is released onto the outside of the anthers and is brushed against insects which enter the flower. The insect then transfers the pollen to the stigma of another or the same flower.
- The **filament** is the stalk which holds up the anther.
- The **sepals** are green petal-like parts which protect the flower while it is growing from a bud into a flower.
- The **receptacle** is the part of the flower which is attached to the stalk. Sometimes, after fertilisation, this becomes part of the fruit; for example, a strawberry.
- The **female** reproductive organs of a plant include the stigma, style and ovary. The pistil is the collective name for the carpel. (Each carpel includes an ovary, a style and a stigma.)
- The **stigma** is the sticky part at the top of the pistil where the pollen adheres during fertilisation.
- The **style** is a tube at the top of the ovary which holds up the stigma and helps to prevent pollen contamination. The style leads down to the **ovary** containing ovules. The **ovary** sometimes becomes the fruit after fertilisation. The ovule becomes the seed.

ANSWERS:

1. 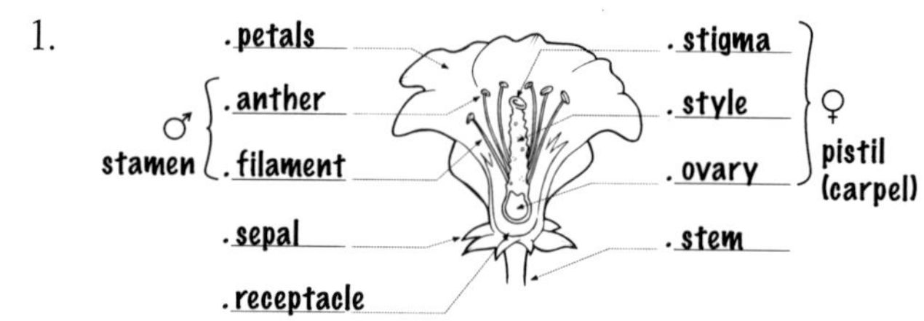

2.

male parts	female parts	other
anther	stigma	petals
filament	style	sepals
	ovary	receptacle
		stem

3. (a) stamen (b) pistil (carpel)

ADDITIONAL ACTIVITIES TO DEVELOP THIS SKILL:

- Construct a large model of the parts of a flower using a range of materials. Use the model to demonstrate the flower parts to pupils in another class.
- Design a crossword puzzle with the flower parts as the answers. Test the puzzle on your friends.
- Play 'Draw as I say' with a friend. Give a friend instructions for drawing a cross-section of a flower showing all its parts. Test your instructions on yourself first to make sure they are easy to follow.

CURRICULUM LINKS

Country	Subject	Level	Objectives
England	Science	KS 2	• Know about the parts of the flower and their role in the lifecycle of flowering plants.
Northern Ireland	Science	KS 2	• Know the main stages in the lifecycle of living things.
Republic of Ireland	Science	3rd/4th Class	• Become aware of some of the basic life processes.
Scotland	Science	Level B/C	• Identify the main parts of flowering plants and their broad functions.
Wales	Science	KS 2	• Know the main stages in the lifecycle of flowering plants.

Parts of a flower

> **Task**
> You will demonstrate that you know the different parts of a flower.

The flower is the section of a plant which contains the reproductive parts. These parts are found in all flowers from different species of plant.

1. Label the parts of the flower.

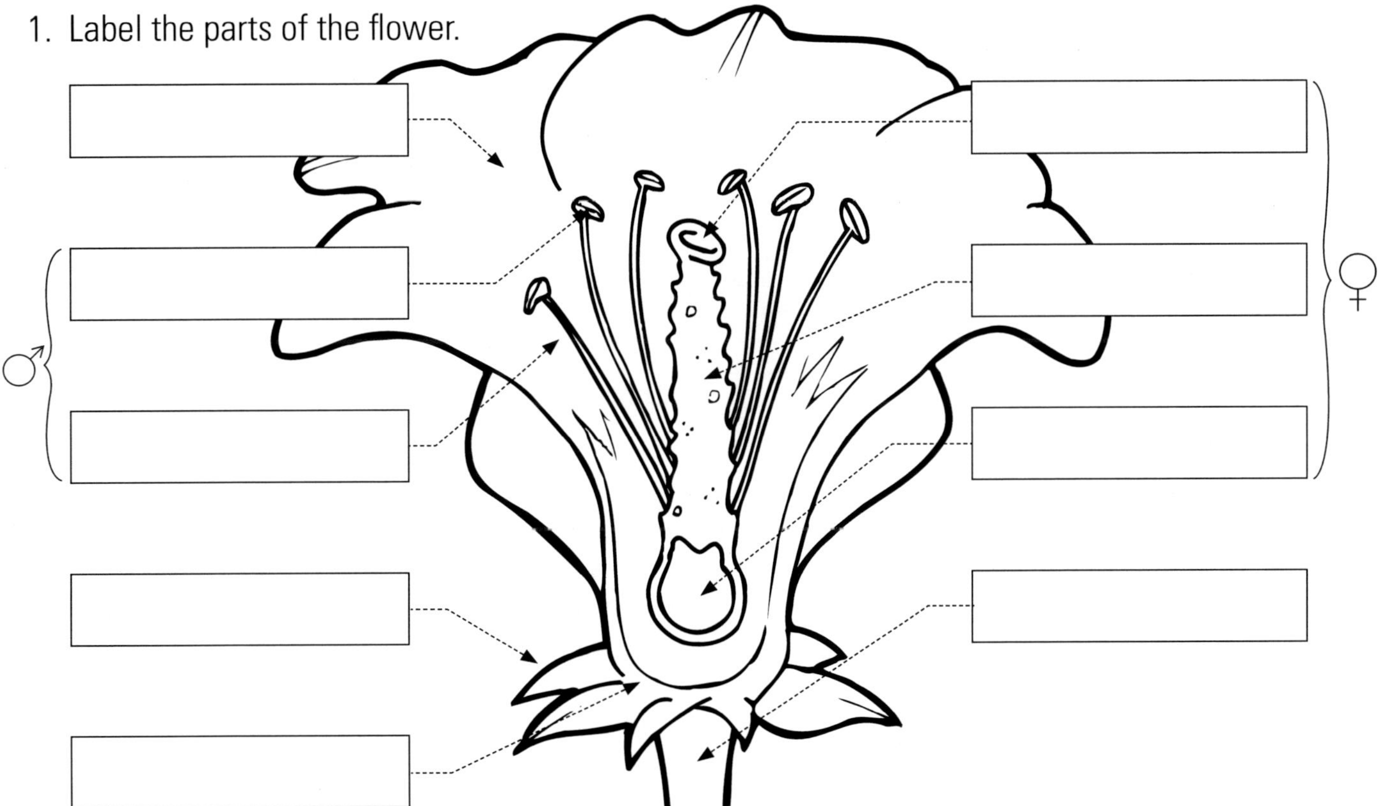

2. Complete the table.

Male parts	Female parts	Other

3. Write the collective name for:

(a) The *male* reproductive organs _______________________________

(b) The *female* reproductive organs _______________________________

> **THINKING MORE ABOUT THINKING**
> What techniques could you use to remember all the different parts of the flower?

Teachers notes

REMEMBERING

> **The skill of remembering demonstrates the pupil's ability to recall information, ideas, data or principles he/she has previously learnt.**

OBJECTIVES:

- Identifies famous natural and human-made landmarks.
- Recalls information about famous world landmarks.

TEACHER INFORMATION:

- For Question 2, encourage the pupils to choose places they have visited. They can then close their eyes and imagine themselves at each location to help them remember the sights, smells, sounds and feelings they may have experienced, in addition to any factual information they can recall.
- After the pupil activities have been completed, the answers can be shared with the class. Any factual information can also be checked using resources such as encyclopedias.

ANSWERS:

1. (a) The Eiffel Tower
   (b) The Great Barrier Reef
   (c) Sydney Opera House
   (d) Mount Everest
   (e) The Taj Mahal
   (f) The Grand Canyon
2. Teacher check

ADDITIONAL ACTIVITIES TO DEVELOP THIS SKILL:

- Design symbols or logos that represent different local landscape features, based on recalled facts.
- Compile class 'fact books' about significant features of their country, based on information recalled by the pupils.
- Divide the class into groups and challenge them to name as many tourist attractions in their country as possible.

CURRICULUM LINKS

Country	Subject	Level	Objectives
England	Geography	KS 2	• Identify places.
Northern Ireland	Geography	KS 2	• Study a range of places.
Republic of Ireland	Geography	3rd/4th Class	• Be aware of human and natural features of other parts of the world.
Scotland	Society	Level C	• Identify world features and locations.
Wales	Geography	KS 2	• Identify places.

World landmarks

Task
You will identify and recall information about famous world landmarks.

There are many famous natural and human-made landmarks in the world.

1. Match each picture below to its correct name.

- *The Eiffel Tower*
- *Sydney Opera House*
- *The Taj Mahal*
- *The Great Barrier Reef*
- *Mount Everest*
- *The Grand Canyon*

2. Choose two of these famous landmarks or two others you have visited or read about. For each, list words or phrases you associate with it; e.g. its location, colour, significance, history.

Landmark 1 ....

Landmark 2 ....

THINKING MORE ABOUT THINKING
Do you find picture or word 'memory joggers' more useful when you are trying to recall something? How well did you remember places you had visited or read about? What kinds of memories stand out for you—things you have seen, touched, smelt, tasted, heard or felt?

REMEMBERING

> The skill of remembering demonstrates the pupil's ability to recall information, ideas, data or principles he/she has previously learnt.

OBJECTIVES:

- Writes song lyrics to show knowledge of basic daily healthy food requirements.
- Completes song lyrics to show the importance of drinking water.

TEACHER INFORMATION:

- The song 'On the first day of Christmas …' has been used as a general format for Question 1. Pupils are not expected to repeat information from the previous verse as is usually done for this song.
- Pupils use the table to record their ideas then write the words to their selected rhymes or songs for Question 2 on the back of the worksheet.

ANSWERS:

Teacher check

ADDITIONAL ACTIVITIES TO DEVELOP THIS SKILL:

- Identify healthy foods from the main food groups which have been included in a menu from the school canteen.
- Name the benefits for overall health which can be gained from eating well.
- Relate healthy foods which have been included in your daily diet.
- Describe how food from each group provides daily health requirements in the form of vitamins and minerals or benefits to tissues, organs and bones etc.
- Discuss the nutritional information from a panel on food from healthy food groups such as packaged cereals or dairy products.
- From each food group record favourite foods eaten by class members on a regular basis.
- Use a graph, table or pictorial representation to show how many servings from each healthy food group should be eaten daily.

CURRICULUM LINKS

Country	Subject	Level	Objectives
England	PSHE	KS 2	• Know what makes a healthy lifestyle, including healthy eating.
Northern Ireland	PD	KS 2	• Understand the benefits of a healthy lifestyle, including healthy eating.
Republic of Ireland	SPHE	3rd/4th Class	• Differentiate between a healthy and an unhealthy diet and appreciate the role of balance and moderation.
Scotland	Health	Level C	• Show their knowledge and understanding of what they do to keep healthy; e.g. choosing nutritious food.
Wales	PSE	KS 2	• Understand the need for a variety of food.

Healthy songs and rhymes

> **Task**
> *You will complete rhymes to show knowledge of healthy diet requirements.*

Songs and rhymes can help us to remember and recall information.

1. Complete the words to this familiar song to show what a healthy daily diet would involve.

   (a) 'For the first meal of the day, my mother gave to me … _________________________

   ____

   ____ ,

   (b) 'For the first snack of the day, my mother gave to me … ________________________

   ____

   ____ ,

   (c) 'For the second meal of the day, my mother gave to me … ______________________

   ____

   ____ ,

   (d) 'For the second snack of the day, my mother gave to me … _____________________

   ____

   ____ ,

   (e) 'For the main meal of the day, my mother gave to me … ________________________

   ____

   ____ ,

2. Change the words of a popular rhyme or song you know to tell why it is important to drink water every day and how much to drink. Use the table for planning then write your rhyme or song on the back of the worksheet.

Name of ***chosen*** song or rhyme:
Name of **your** song or rhyme:
Ideas *(keywords)*:

THINKING MORE ABOUT THINKING
Did you manage to include all the main food groups in Question 1? How could rhymes like this help you to remember information or facts in other topics? Which learning areas would suit this method of remembering?

THINKING SKILLS

Teachers notes
REMEMBERING

> The skill of remembering demonstrates the pupil's ability to recall information, ideas, data or principles which he/she has previously learnt.

OBJECTIVES:

- Identifies elements of a story with specific music and movement.
- Relates story using music and movement score.

TEACHER INFORMATION:

- Using a range of resources when telling a story increases the chance of more pupils picking up more information from the text.
- Pupils discuss their combined memories of the chosen story and work together to complete the task. They perform the story with narrators to read the full text, 'dancers' to perform character movements and 'musicians' to play the percussion instruments effectively.

ANSWERS:

Teacher check

ADDITIONAL ACTIVITIES TO DEVELOP THIS SKILL:

- Study the number of different ways each percussion instrument can be used and the type of atmosphere and movement each could be used to illustrate. Present your research in a table.
- Research how the use of light and colour could further enhance the performance of storytelling.
- Use a range of art skills and materials to make durable face masks for each character in a story.

CURRICULUM LINKS

Country	Subject	Level	Objectives
England	English	KS 2	• Use character, action and narrative to convey story and emotions in plays.
Northern Ireland	English	KS 2	• Improvise a scene based on literature.
Republic of Ireland	English	3rd/4th Class	• Dramatise stories.
Scotland	Drama	Level C	• Be involved in imaginative drama such as narrative fiction.
Wales	English	KS 2	• Participate in a wide range of drama activities.

Performance

> ***Task***
> *You will use music and movement to interest the*
> *audience and help them to remember a story.*

Stories can be brought to life by using music and movement. The instruments used, the way they are played and the movement of the actors' bodies can breathe life into a simple script.

1. (a) In groups, choose a familiar short story to work on.

   (b) Discuss how the feelings of each character change throughout the story and how these will be shown through music and movement.

   (c) Discuss how the atmosphere of the story changes from scene to scene and how you will use percussion instruments to illustrate this.

2. Complete the tables, using extra paper if needed.

   (a) ***Characters***

character	feeling	movement	music

   (b) ***Atmosphere***

scene	atmosphere	music

3. (a) Perform your story for the rest of the class.

   (b) How well do you think your performance was received?

   cold   cool   warm   hot   scorching

Thinking challenges 1

Remembering	• On a copy of a world map, locate and colour where the Inuit live. Describe the climate of the region. • Use a word web to record information about their traditional lifestyle.
Understanding	• Explain how the climate of the region affects their lifestyle. • Find materials to make clothes for an Inuit doll.
Applying	• Make a museum booklet describing the traditional Inuit way of life, including pictures and sketches. • Play the role of a tour guide and present the information to your group.
Analysing	• Choose an animal hunted by the Inuit and use a word web to illustrate how they used all parts of the animal to support their lifestyle. • Present your information as a television documentary programme.
Evaluating	• Compare the old and modern Inuit lifestyles. • Dramatise a conversation between an old Inuit person and a young one, arguing about which way of life is better.
Creating	• Travel 200 years back in time. Write four entries in a journal for a week spent with an Inuit family in each season. Illustrate your journal with informative sketches.

Topic focus   **Marsupials**

Remembering	• Design an illustrated chart of Australian marsupials. • On a map of Australia, indicate where each can be found.
Understanding	• Make an illustrated booklet for younger pupils, explaining what a marsupial is.
Applying	• Make a model of a marsupial with all body parts in the correct proportion.
Analysing	• Present a 'wildlife programme' in which you explain in detail the lifecycle and habits of one marsupial. Use a word web for organising your information.
Evaluating	• Compare the similarities and differences between marsupials. Use a graphic organiser to present your information.
Creating	• Write a poem describing all aspects of a marsupial. • Write clues for a, 'Which marsupial am I?' crossword. • Write question and answer cards for a marsupial quiz. • Create a marsupial word search.

UNDERSTANDING

Pupil checklist		
Aesop's fables	Pages 20–21	❑
Favourite films	Pages 22–23	❑
Food chains	Pages 24–25	❑
From farm to table	Pages 26–27	❑
All about bullying	Pages 28–29	❑
Bulletin board	Pages 30–31	❑

UNDERSTANDING: PUPIL SELF-EVALUATION

Use the sections below to record thoughts or information about the worksheets or answers to the metacognitive questions on each pupil page.

Name ....

| Pages 20–21 | Aesop's fables |

| Pages 22–23 | Favourite films |

| Pages 24–25 | Food chains |

| Pages 26–27 | From farm to table |

| Pages 28–29 | All about bullying |

| Pages 30–31 | Bulletin board |

UNDERSTANDING

Pages	Title	Key learning areas	Thinking activity
20–21	Aesop's fables	English	• Identifies the moral of chosen fables. • Interprets the personalities and character types portrayed by animals in chosen fables.
22–23	Favourite films	Mathematics	• Interprets information presented as a bar chart.
24–25	Food chains	Science	• Completes diagrams of two food chains.
26–27	From farm to table	Geography	• Organises knowledge to complete a milk processing flow chart. • Explains the need for heat treatment and correct storage of milk products.
28–29	All about bullying	Health/Values	• Identifies examples of physical, social and verbal bullying. • Understands some of the benefits of dealing with bullying assertively.
30–31	Bulletin board	Art	• Explains why particular images have been used in an advertising billboard.

DEFINITION:

The skill of *understanding* involves explaining what has been learnt in a different way to show the level of comprehension. This may be done in a number of ways, including interpreting the material and summarising it, delivering the material to a different audience, using concrete resources and presenting a brief talk.

SOME APPROPRIATE VERBS:

interpret, summarise, infer, paraphrase, give examples, explain, sequence, sort, match, classify, locate, collect, compare and measure, restate, discuss, express, give in your own words, identify, report, review, select, clarify, illustrate, describe, predict.

SOME APPROPRIATE GRAPHIC ORGANISERS:

Mind map, PMI, Venn diagram, Cycle, Compare or contrast chart, T-chart, Concept chart, Chains, Categories chart, Tree, Matrix etc.

SOME SUITABLE QUESTIONS:

Can you write in your own words … ?, How would you explain … ?, Can you give a brief outline … ?, What could have happened next?, Who do you think … ?, What was the main idea?, Why did the character act this way? etc.

Teachers notes

UNDERSTANDING

> **The skill of understanding involves explaining what has been learnt in a different way to show the level of comprehension.**

OBJECTIVES:

- Identifies the moral of chosen fables.
- Interprets the personalities and character types portrayed by animal characters in chosen fables.

TEACHER INFORMATION:

- It is important for pupils to express, in their own words, the lessons delivered by Aesop's fables, as this demonstrates their level of understanding of the moral. Some fables may have only one message to give but others may be interpreted in a number of ways.
- Recognising different personalities and character traits helps pupils understand why particular animals were chosen to illustrate the moral of the story. This enhances their understanding of the moral.

ANSWERS:

Teacher check

ADDITIONAL ACTIVITIES TO DEVELOP THIS SKILL:

- Make a booklet introducing the main characters of a selection of fables. Describe the personality and character of each.
- Make a display of positive behaviours learnt from a selection of fables.
- In groups, dramatise a chosen fable. Rewrite the story in script form, ending with a positive affirmation of the moral.

CURRICULUM LINKS

Country	Subject	Level	Objectives
England	English	KS 2	• Read traditional stories and identify how character and themes are developed.
Northern Ireland	Language and literacy	KS 2	• Read traditional texts and discuss themes, characters and plots.
Republic of Ireland	English	3rd/4th Class	• Experience different types of text and engage in talk; e.g. plot, character.
Scotland	English	Level C	• Read fiction and comment on characters' behaviour and reasons.
Wales	English	KS 2	• Read traditional stories and respond to plot, characters and ideas.

www.prim-ed.com • Prim-Ed Publishing

Aesop's fables

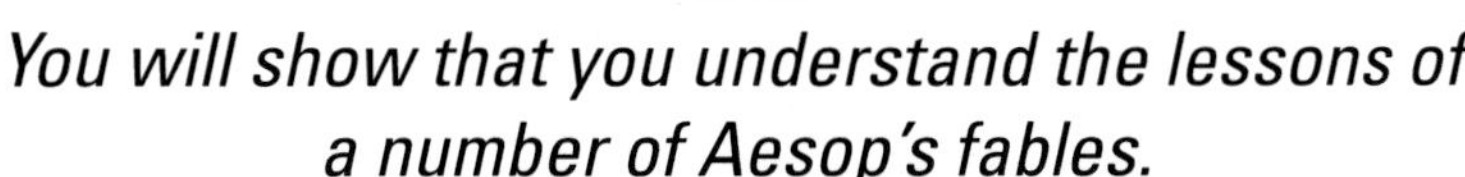
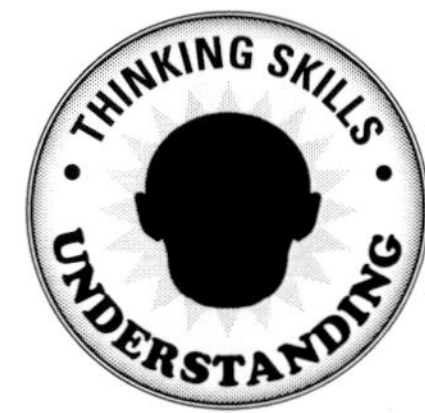

> ***Task***
> *You will show that you understand the lessons of*
> *a number of Aesop's fables.*

Aesop was a legendary Greek slave who lived in the 6th century BCE. His fables are stories which teach a lesson. They were passed down by word of mouth for 200 years before they were written down. The lessons tell about human strengths and weaknesses.

1. (a) In groups, choose four of Aesop's fables to discuss. Then write the lesson to be learnt for each fable below.

fable	lesson

   (b) Choose one fable to act out for the rest of the class.

2. Aesop used animals in many of his stories to show particular personalities and character types. From a selection of Aesop's fables, choose four animals and write words and phrases to describe how the fables portray each.

animal	personality/character traits

> ***THINKING MORE ABOUT THINKING***
> *How did this activity help you to understand each fable? How will you*
> *use your understanding of Aesop's fables to help you when you are in a*
> *difficult situation?*

Teachers notes

UNDERSTANDING

The skill of understanding involves explaining what has been learnt in a different way to show the level of comprehension.

OBJECTIVE:

- Interprets information presented as a bar chart.

TEACHER INFORMATION:

- The pupils will need to be familiar with the conventions of bar charts before completing this activity.

ANSWERS:

1. Answers will vary, but should be similar to the following: 'Favourite films of teenagers'.
2. seven
3. (a) comedy   (b) 15
4. (a) drama   (b) 2
5. Yes – sci-fi, fantasy and horror
6. 58
7. Teacher check

ADDITIONAL ACTIVITIES TO DEVELOP THIS SKILL:

- Interpret a range of graphical representations; e.g. Venn diagrams, two-way tables, pictograms etc.
- Give a written explanation of the information contained in a graph.
- Construct a bar chart that summarises given information.

CURRICULUM LINKS

Country	Subject	Level	Objectives
England	Maths	KS 2	• Interpret data using graphs, including bar charts.
Northern Ireland	Maths and numeracy	KS 2	• Interpret a wide range of graphs.
Republic of Ireland	Maths	3rd/4th Class	• Read and interpret bar charts.
Scotland	Maths	Level C	• Interpret data from displays.
Wales	Maths	KS 2	• Interpret a wide range of graphs.

Favourite films

> **Task**
> *You will answer questions about a bar chart.*

A number of teenagers were asked to name their favourite type of film. Their answers are shown in the bar chart below.

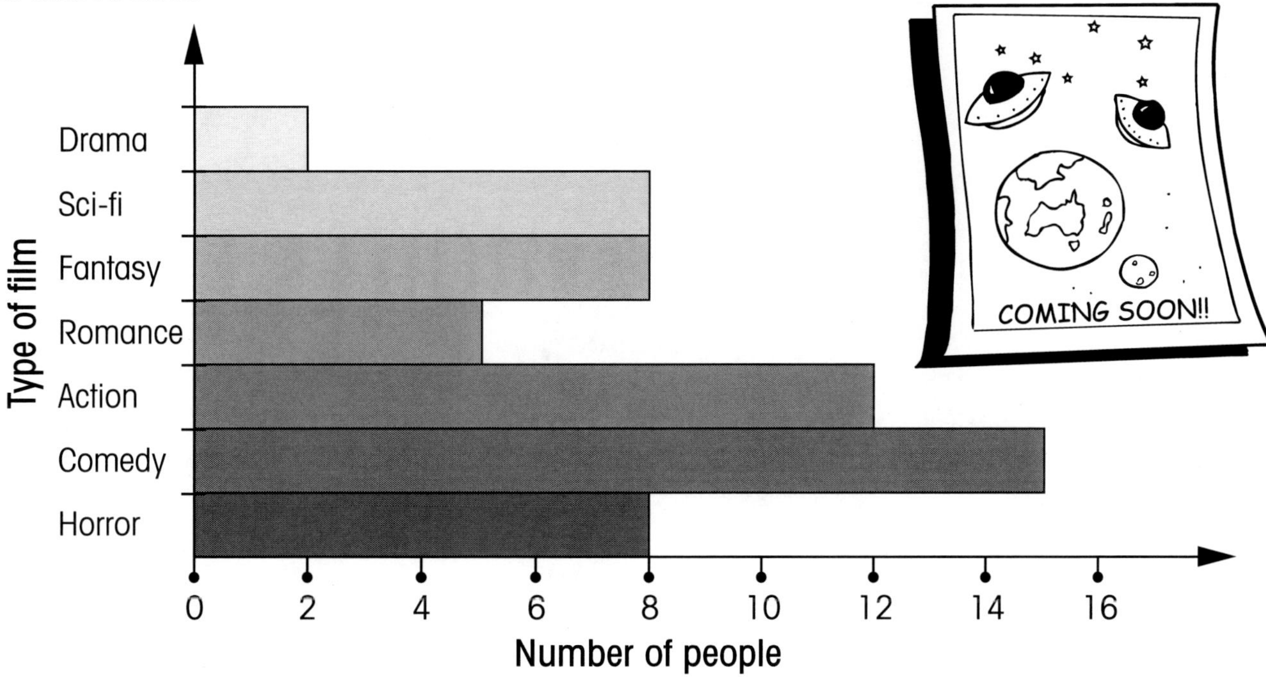

Answer the questions below.

1. Write a suitable title for this bar chart.

   ____

2. How many types of films are shown on the bar chart? _________

3. (a) Which was the most popular type of film? _______________________

   (b) How many people enjoyed this the most? _________

4. (a) Which was the least popular type of film? _______________________

   (b) How many people enjoyed this the most? _________

5. Were any of the scores the same for more than one film type? (((Yes No)))

   If yes, which? ____

6. How many people in total took part in the survey? _________

7. Which type of film from the bar chart is your favourite? _______________________

THINKING MORE ABOUT THINKING
How easy do you find bar charts to understand? How do they compare with other types of graphs? Would the information presented in the bar chart on this page have been better presented in a different format? Which question(s) was/were the most difficult to answer? Why?

Teachers notes

UNDERSTANDING

> **The skill of understanding involves explaining what has been learnt in a different way to show the level of comprehension.**

OBJECTIVE:

- Completes diagrams of two food chains.

TEACHER INFORMATION:

- Pupils are required to demonstrate understanding of simple food chains.

- Food chains show how each living thing gets its food. Some animals eat plants and others eat animals. Each link in a food chain is food for the next link in the chain. Food chains start with plant life and end with an animal. Some food chains include the sun as the first source of energy. Others include the terms *producers* (plants are called producers because they use energy from the sun to produce food from carbon dioxide and water), *consumers* (animals are the main consumers — herbivores, carnivores and omnivores) and *decomposers* (bacteria and fungi feed on decaying matter and provide food for plants). Most food chains have no more than four or five links. Animals may be a part of more than one food chain because they eat more than one kind of food to survive. The connection between the food chains forms a food web. Food chains can be affected when one or more elements are affected, such as clearing areas of land of plants.

ANSWERS:

Teacher check.

(Some possible food chains are given below.)

Trees are eaten by giraffes. Giraffes are eaten by lions. So a simple food chain would be:

trees ➪ giraffes ➪ lions

A more complex food chain would be:

grass ➪ grasshopper ➪ frog ➪ snake ➪ hawk

ADDITIONAL ACTIVITIES TO DEVELOP THIS SKILL:

- Explain the meaning of 'food chain' in your own words.

- Interpret a diagram showing a food chain and explain how the diagram accurately and concisely shows the way the food chain works.

- Locate a food chain similar to those given to complete the worksheet and find similarities and differences.

- Compare the number of links in one food chain with those in another.

- Classify animals on a food chain into herbivores, carnivores and omnivores.

- Sort a list of plants and animals into producers, consumers and decomposers.

- Match the same animals in different food chains and show why they have been included.

- Describe two examples of food chains in your own words for the class.

CURRICULUM LINKS

Country	Subject	Level	Objectives
England	Science	KS 2	• Use food chains to show feeding relationships in a habitat and know that nearly all food chains start with a green plant.
Northern Ireland	Science	KS 2	• Know about the relationship between animals and plants in a habitat.
Republic of Ireland	Science	3rd/4th Class	• Appreciate that animals depend on plants and indirectly on the sun for food and discuss simple food chains.
Scotland	Science	Level B	• Give examples of feeding relationships found in the local environment and construct simple food chains.
Wales	Science	KS 2	• Know that food chains show feeding relationships in an ecosystem and that nearly all food chains start with a green plant.

Food chains

Task
You will show understanding of two specific food chains.

In the spaces below, explain how two different food chains work. Label all parts of the chain and use appropriate boxes or drawings and arrows.

Food chain on the land

Food chain in the sea

UNDERSTANDING

> **The skill of understanding involves explaining what has been learnt in a different way to show the level of comprehension.**

OBJECTIVES:

- Organises knowledge to complete a milk processing flow chart.
- Explains the need for heat treatment and correct storage of milk and its products.

TEACHER INFORMATION:

- Using a flow chart to demonstrate a process breaks information into manageable parts, making the process easier to understand. Any part in the process may then be highlighted for further research and discussion.
- Milk products are made using pasteurised milk. Some milks which can be found in non-refrigerated aisles in a supermarket have been ultra heat treated. UHT kills both pathogenic and spoilage organisms, increasing the product's shelf life and removing the need for refrigeration until the seal is broken.

ANSWERS:

1. Answers will vary but may be similar to the following.

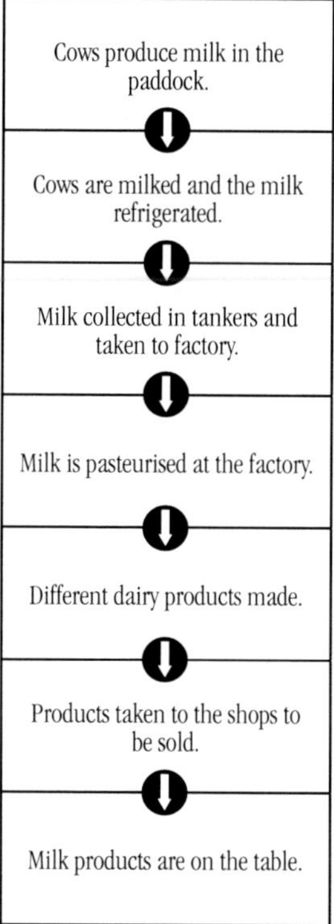

2. (a) Heat treatment; i.e. pasteurisation.

   (b) To kill germs (pathogenic organisms).

3. (a) In refrigerated conditions.

   (b) They will go 'off'.

4. Dairy products: up to a few weeks.

   Dried foods: for many months.

ADDITIONAL ACTIVITIES TO DEVELOP THIS SKILL:

- Research the manufacturing process for specific dairy products; e.g. cottage cheese, yogurt, cream. Present information in a flow chart.
- Compare the nutrition information of:

   (a) different types of the same food; e.g. whole milk, skimmed milk, hi-calcium, low fat milk.

   (b) different dairy foods; e.g. cheese, yogurt, butter.

   Present information in a comparison chart.

- Research the different types of heat treatment for milk. Use a comparison chart to present information.

CURRICULUM LINKS

Country	Subject	Level	Objectives
England	Geography	KS 2	• Recognise human processes and interdependence of places; e.g. supply of goods.
Northern Ireland	Geography	KS 2	• Know about jobs associated with the provision of goods and the journey of a product from raw material to consumer.
Republic of Ireland	Geography	3rd/4th Class	• Explore common economic activities; e.g. food and farming.
Scotland	Society	Level D	• Describe features of economic life; e.g. farming.
Wales	Geography	KS 2	• Extend geographical vocabulary; e.g. farming and know how localities link to other localities; e.g. supply of goods.

From farm to table

> **Task**
> *You will show that you understand the milk process, from cows in the paddock to dairy foods in your refrigerator.*

The main ingredient in all dairy products is milk. Most of the milk consumed comes from cows, with a very small percentage coming from goats and sheep. In milk processing factories around the country, many different dairy products are made and then transported to shops and supermarkets.

1. Complete the flow chart to show the journey of milk and its products from paddock to table.

   Cows produce milk in the paddock

   ↓

   ↓

   ↓

   ↓

   ↓

   ↓

   Milk products are on the table.

2. (a) What important treatment does milk receive at the factory before it is processed?

   (b) Why is this treatment necessary?

3. (a) How should dairy foods be stored?

   (b) What happens if dairy foods are not stored correctly?

4. Compare the longest use-by dates you can find on two dairy products and two dried foods such as packet soup or pasta.

Dairy product	Use by date

Dried food	Use by date

THINKING MORE ABOUT THINKING
How did using the flow chart help you understand the dairy process? In what other situations would you find a flow chart useful?

Teachers notes

UNDERSTANDING

> **The skill of understanding involves explaining what has been learnt in a different way to show the level of comprehension.**

OBJECTIVES:

- Identifies examples of physical, social and verbal bullying.
- Understands some of the benefits of dealing with bullying assertively.

TEACHER INFORMATION:

- Most definitions of bullying agree:
  - It is deliberately hurtful (physically or psychologically).
  - It is repeated often over time.
  - It is difficult for the person being bullied to defend himself/herself against it. (He/She is weaker physically or psychologically.)
- The worksheet suggests some assertive ways of tackling bullying. Assertive people show respect for others and themselves equally. The pupils should avoid acting passively or aggressively in response to bullying and should be encouraged to tell an adult about the problem if they cannot deal with it themselves.

ANSWERS:

1. (a) P, S
   (b) V, S
   (c) P
   (d) V, S
2. Teacher check

ADDITIONAL ACTIVITIES TO DEVELOP THIS SKILL:

- Discuss how people who are bullied might feel.
- Make a list of reasons why people might bully.
- Have the pupils give examples of different types of bullying they have experienced or witnessed.
- Categorise conflict scenarios into those that are bullying and those that are not.
- Identify examples of bullying on television.

CURRICULUM LINKS

Country	Subject	Level	Objectives
England	PSHE	KS 2	• Realise the nature of bullying and how to respond.
Northern Ireland	PD	KS 2	• Recognise the nature of bullying.
Republic of Ireland	SPHE	3rd/4th Class	• Recognise and explore ways of dealing with bullying.
Scotland	Health	Level C	• Show safe ways of dealing with bullying situations.
Wales	PSE	KS 2	• Develop strategies to deal with bullying.

All about bullying

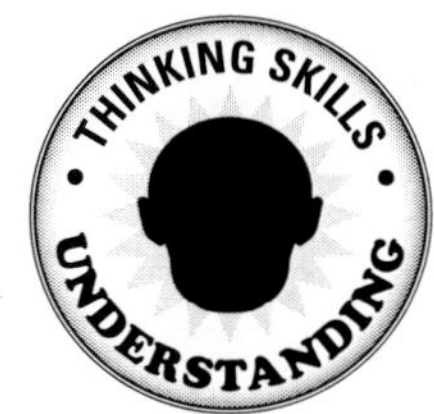

> ***Task***
> *You will understand what bullying is and some*
> *positive ways to deal with it.*

Bullying is deliberately hurting other people with words or actions. Bullying can be physical (e.g. hitting or scratching someone), social (e.g. leaving people out or putting people down) or verbal (e.g. name-calling or teasing).

1. Read the school bullying situations below. Sort them by letter into the correct type—
P *(physical)*, S *(social)* or V *(verbal)*. Some may belong to more than one type.

   (a) A group of girls trip Ella whenever she walks by.

   (b) Jack spreads nasty rumours about Tom, causing other pupils to ignore him.

   (c) Every morning, Bridget is stopped at the school gate by
   Grace, who pinches her and takes her lunch money.

   (d) Nicholas, a new pupil, asks to sit with a group of boys at
   lunchtime, but they call him names and run away.

2. (a) Many people feel helpless when they are being bullied, but there are some things you can
   do in any bullying situation. Read these pieces of advice.

   > • *Appear calm and confident – even if you have to pretend. Say firmly, 'I don't like what you are doing. I want you to stop'.*
   > • *Get away from the situation – find friends or a safe place.*
   > • *Tell an adult if you feel you can't deal with the problem yourself.*

   (b) Answer these questions.

   (i)   Why might appearing confident be a good way to deal with bullying?

   ____

   ____

   (ii) List three 'safe places' you could go to get away from bullying.

   ____

   (iii) Give an example of something an adult might do to help.

   ____

   ____

THINKING MORE ABOUT THINKING
How did you decide which category/categories the situations belonged to for Question 1? Did you picture scenarios in your head to answer Question 2 or did you use another method?

UNDERSTANDING

> **The skill of understanding involves explaining what has been learnt in a different way to show the level of comprehension.**

OBJECTIVE:

- Explains why particular images have been used in an advertising billboard.

TEACHER INFORMATION:

- This activity aims to help pupils identify ways visual art is used in contemporary society in areas such as advertising. Pupils should understand that images are chosen which appeal to the intended audience. Language is used which is relevant to that audience. Both the images and the language show that advertisers give careful thought to the particular market.

ANSWERS:

Teacher check

ADDITIONAL ACTIVITIES TO DEVELOP THIS SKILL:

- Explain why the advertiser chose to sell jeans to young adults.
- Review a television commercial advertising jeans. Explain why the images and language were chosen. Were they successful or not at encouraging the target audience to buy the jeans?
  - ~ Express your opinion about the images and language used.
  - ~ Discuss why images such as those used in this advertisement are often used in advertising.
  - ~ Describe the stereotypes used in the jeans advertisement.
- Collect examples of similar advertisements in magazines or newspapers for display.
- Classify the various components of each advertisement; for example, headline, image, body text.

CURRICULUM LINKS

Country	Subject	Level	Objectives
England	Art and design	KS 2	• Record from experience and imagination and explore ideas for different purposes.
Northern Ireland	Art and design	KS 2	• Investigate and respond to experience, memory and imagination.
Republic of Ireland	Visual arts	3rd/4th Class	• Make drawings from experience, imagination and observation.
Scotland	Art and design	Level C	• Create images in response to things which have been observed, experienced or imagined.
Wales	Art	KS 2	• Select and record from observation, experience and imagination.

Bulletin board

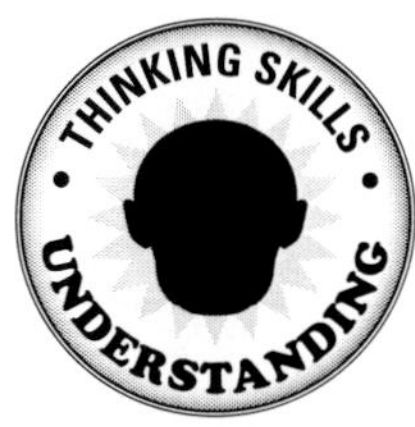

> ### Task
> *You will explain about the image used on an advertising billboard for a popular brand of jeans.*

1. Look at the billboard below and answer the questions.

2. What is the advertiser trying to say by using the image that he/she has?

____

____

____

____

____

____

____

____

____

____

____

____

3. What do the words at the *bottom* of the billboard mean?

____

____

____

4. What other images could have been used to advertise the jeans? Write or draw some on the back of the worksheet and explain why these images would be good to use.

THINKING MORE ABOUT THINKING
Share your answers with a partner. How are his/her answers similar to or different from yours? Why? How could you have improved your answers?

Thinking challenges 2

Remembering	• Record as much information as you can about the pyramids of Ancient Egypt.
Understanding	• Draw and label a diagram of a pyramid. • Explain why Pharaohs were buried in pyramids. • Describe how pyramids were constructed.
Applying	• Use the information about pyramids to create an elaborate tomb for the king of a fictitious country.
Analysing	• Give reasons why pyramids have endured. • Give your own opinion about pyramids. Are they marvels of building or monstrosities?
Evaluating	• Suggest ways you could improve a pyramid if you were building one today.
Creating	• Design, plan and create a model of a pyramid. • Write a narrative about a slave working on the building of a pyramid.

Topic focus   **Superheroes**

Remembering	• List as many superheroes as you can and write details about them.
Understanding	• Use a table to show similarities and differences between a number of superheroes. • Draw labelled illustrations to show how superheroes create or use their superhero skills.
Applying	• Write a list of reasons why it may be better for superheroes to keep their identity a secret.
Analysing	• Organise two lists of superheroes—one for those who inherited their powers from their parents and one for those who acquired them by accident.
Evaluating	• List the advantages and disadvantages of being a superhero and decide whether you would like to be one or not.
Creating	• Create a new superhero. Describe his/her superhero talents and how they were obtained. Describe your superhero's appearance and how his/her super talents and identity are hidden from the world.

APPLYING

APPLYING: PUPIL SELF-EVALUATION

Use the sections below to record thoughts or information about the worksheets or answers to the metacognitive questions on each pupil page.

Name

Pages 36–37	**Black mamba**

Pages 38–39	**Classifying shapes**

Pages 40–41	**Gliding away …**

Pages 42–43	**Community life**

Pages 44–45	**Healthy weekend**

Pages 46–47	**Story sounds**

Teacher introduction
APPLYING

Pages	Title	Key learning areas	Thinking activity
36–37	Black mamba	English	• Identifies errors in a text. • Rewrites text correctly.
38–39	Classifying shapes	Mathematics	• Uses knowledge of geometrical features of simple 2-D shapes to place shapes in the correct place on Venn and Tree diagrams.
40–41	Gliding away …	Science	• Constructs and flies a paper glider according to a set of instructions. • Uses information to make improvements to a paper glider.
42–43	Community life	Geography	• Selects natural and built features for an imaginary community. • Determines the staff and goods and services required by each of the features selected.
44–45	Healthy weekend	Health	• Uses knowledge of healthy lifestyle principles to devise a 'kick-start' plan for an unhealthy friend. • Demonstrates an understanding of difficulties that may be encountered and suggests ideas for support.
46–47	Story sounds	Music	• Uses sound and music to represent the story of Little Red Riding Hood.

DEFINITION:

The skill of applying demonstrates a pupil's ability to USE previously learnt material in a new or familiar situation. It aims to find out whether a pupil is able to explain ideas or concepts. Pupils are able to apply information if they can select, transfer or use data and principles to complete or solve a problem or task with minimal help from the teacher.

SOME APPROPRIATE VERBS AND PHRASES:

implement, carry out, use, ask questions, predict outcomes, define the problem, plan a research, improve ideas, anticipate the consequences, test conclusions, demonstrate, generalise, illustrate, interpret, relate, compute, solve, apply, construct, execute, show etc.

SOME APPROPRIATE GRAPHIC ORGANISERS:

Flow chart, T-chart, Compare or contrast chart, Compare and contrast chart, Venn diagram, Spider map, Fishbone, Cloud/Cluster, Tree etc.

SOME SUITABLE QUESTIONS:

Can you give another example of … ?, Could this have happened when … ?, Which things would you change if … ?, Can you make up a set of questions from the information given?, How would you explain … ?, Does everyone act in the same way … ? etc.

APPLYING

> **The skill of applying demonstrates a pupil's ability to use previously learnt material in a new or familiar situation.**

OBJECTIVES:

- Identifies errors in a text.
- Rewrites text correctly.

TEACHER INFORMATION:

- To edit correctly, pupils need to be able to apply a lot of information about spelling rules, grammar and punctuation to unseen text. Editing requires concentrated thinking.

ANSWERS:

The black mamba is the deadliest snake in the world**.** It's **S**outh Africa's most ***poisonous*** snake**. It** can grow up to lengths of four metres and can travel at ***speeds*** of up ***to*** 19 kilometres per hour**. T**he black mamba gets its name from the inside lining of its mouth, which is purple-black**. It** shows its mouth when it feels threatened**. It** feeds on small ***mammals*** and birds and is able to eat its ***prey*** whole**.**

It likes to sleep in hollow trees or ***holes*** in the ground**. F**emale mambas can lay from six to seventeen eggs which hatch three months later**. B**lack mambas are found in ***pairs*** or small groups**. T**he ***venom*** of the mamba can kill almost anything**.**

Missing punctuation and grammar is in **bold type**. *Spelling errors are in* **italic type**. *(to, prey, holes, pairs, poisonous, speeds, mammals, venom)*

ADDITIONAL ACTIVITIES TO DEVELOP THIS SKILL:

- Improve the text by adding some interesting adjectives and adverbs.
- Use your skills to edit each piece of your writing before publishing.
- Collate words which follow the same spelling rules into a list for referral.
- Illustrate your knowledge of particular spelling rules to spell unfamiliar words during writing sessions.
- Demonstrate your editing skills by reviewing the work of another classmate and offering suggestions.

CURRICULUM LINKS

Country	Subject	Level	Objectives
England	English	KS 2	• Proofread – check for spelling and punctuation errors.
Northern Ireland	Language and literacy	KS 2	• Develop increasing competence in the use of grammar and punctuation and spell words correctly.
Republic of Ireland	English	3rd/4th Class	• Learn to use a wider range of punctuation marks and write with increasing grammatical accuracy through the process of editing.
Scotland	English	Level C	• Use a range of punctuation marks and mark possible spelling errors.
Wales	English	KS 2	• Proofread – check for spelling and punctuation errors.

Black mamba

> **Task**
> *You will use your knowledge of spelling, grammar and punctuation to edit the text.*

1. Circle or highlight any errors in the text.

the black mamba is the deadliest snake in the world its south africas most poisonus snake it can grow up to lengths of four metres and can travel at speads of up too 19 kilometres per hour the black mamba gets its name from the inside lining of its mouth, which is purple-black it shows its mouth when it feels threatened it feeds on small mammels and birds and is able to eat its pray whole it likes to sleep in hollow trees or wholes in the ground female mambas can lay from six to seventeen eggs which hatch three months later black mambas are found in pears or small groups the venim of the mamba can kill almost anything

2. Rewrite the text correctly.

____

____

____

____

____

____

____

____

____

____

____

THINKING MORE ABOUT THINKING

Were you able to find all the errors? Which did you miss? Is there a reason why you missed those particular errors? Are there some editing 'rules' which you may not know? How can you find out these rules?

Teachers notes

APPLYING

> **The skill of applying demonstrates a pupil's ability to use previously learnt material in a new or familiar situation.**

OBJECTIVE:

- Uses knowledge of geometrical features of simple 2-D shapes to place shapes in the correct place on Venn and Tree diagrams.

TEACHER INFORMATION:

- Look at simple 2-D shapes and count the sides and corners; e.g. square, rectangle, triangle, circle, semicircle, pentagon.
- Find harder 2-D shapes, name them and count the sides and corners; e.g. oval, hexagon, octagon.
- Discuss how Venn and Tree diagrams work. Practise sorting 2-D shapes and other objects using them.

ANSWERS:

1. Teacher check

2. 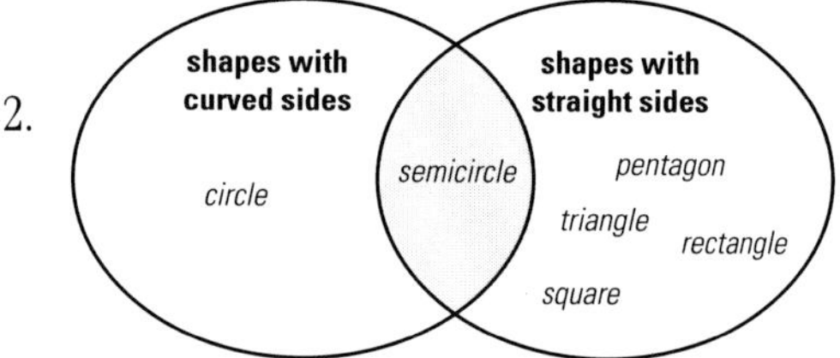

3. semicircle, circle, square, rectangle, pentagon, triangle

ADDITIONAL ACTIVITIES TO DEVELOP THIS SKILL:

- Choose a 2-D shape and write a sentence to describe it.
- Play the 'Feely bag' game. One pupil chooses a 2-D shape, hidden in a bag, and describes it to their partner/ group using only their sense of touch. The partner/group have to guess the shape.
- Sort a collection of 2-D shapes according to different criteria; for example, the number of sides, whether curved etc.
- Place two large hoops on the floor so that they overlap. Use the hoops as a giant Venn diagram to sort shapes and objects according to simple criteria.
- Sort shapes and objects using tree diagrams.

CURRICULUM LINKS

Country	Subject	Level	Objectives
England	Maths	KS 2	• Use geometrical language to describe 2-D shapes and represent data on a range of diagrams.
Northern Ireland	Maths and numeracy	KS 2	• Describe common 2-D shapes and present data on diagrams.
Republic of Ireland	Maths	3rd/4th Class	• Know about the properties of 2-D shapes and represent data on charts.
Scotland	Maths	Level D	• Discuss geometrical features and properties of 2-D shapes and display data on charts.
Wales	Maths	KS 2	• Recognise the geometrical features and properties of 2-D shapes and represent data on a range of diagrams.

Classifying shapes

> **Task**
> *You will write the names of the 2-D shapes in the correct place on the Venn and Tree diagrams.*

1. Look at these shapes.

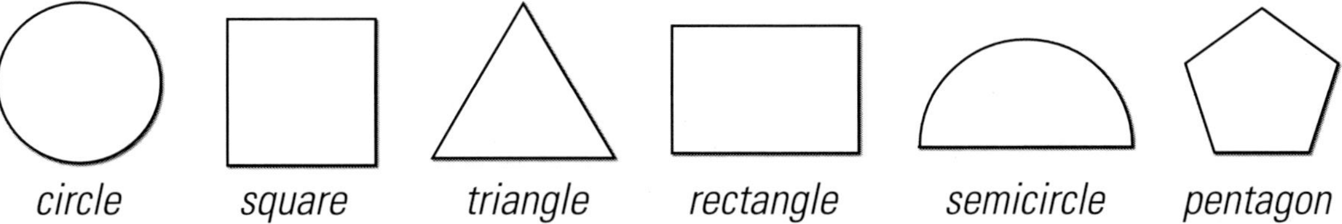

2. Write the names of each shape into the correct place on the Venn diagram.

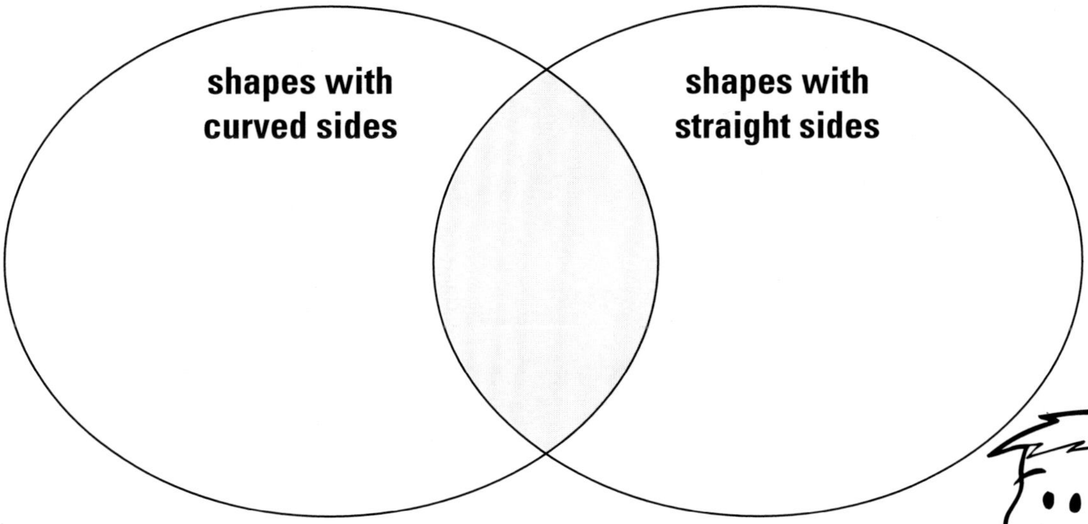

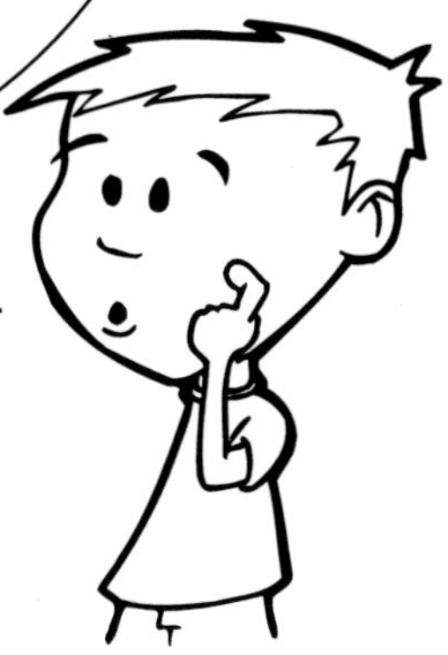

3. Write the names of each shape onto the correct place on the Tree diagram.

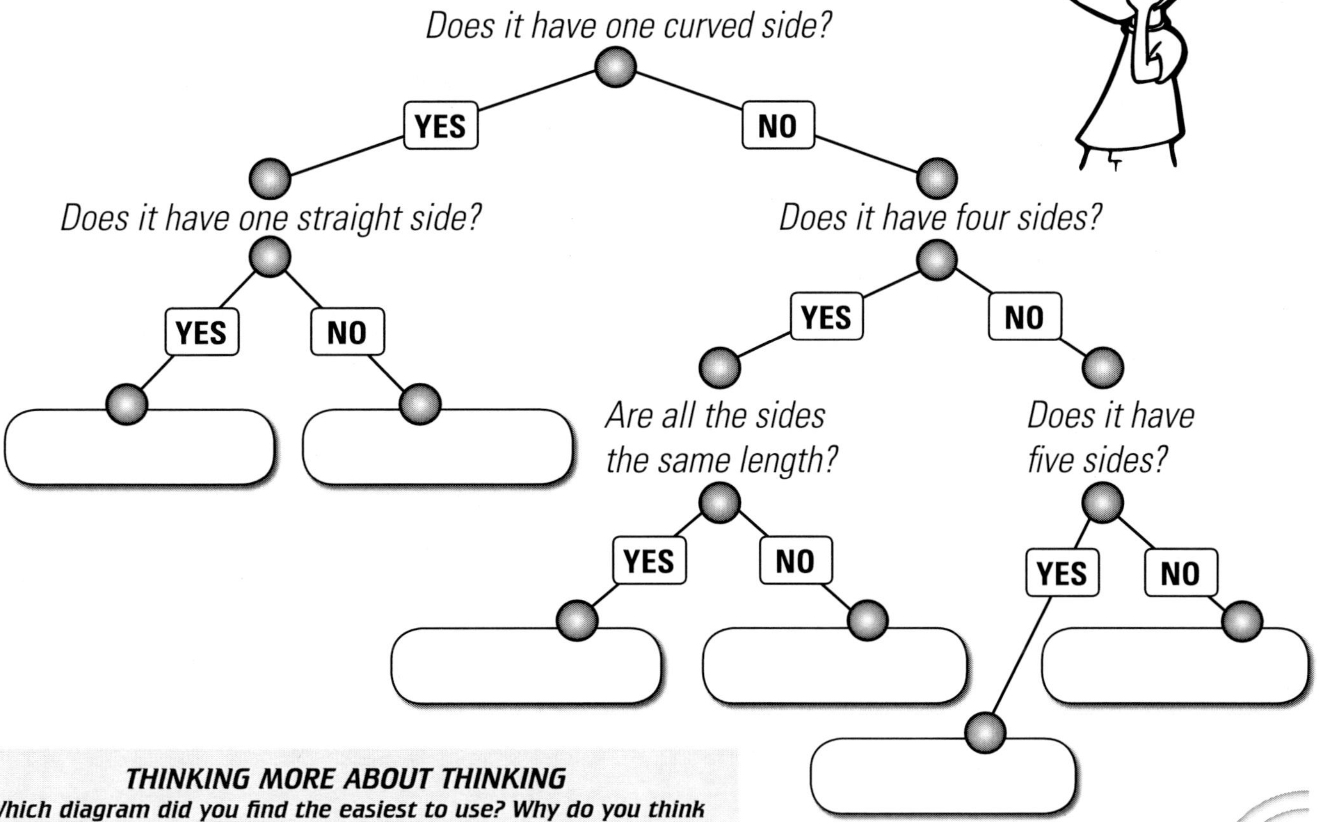

Teachers notes

APPLYING

> The skill of applying demonstrates a pupil's ability to use previously learnt material in a new or familiar situation.

OBJECTIVES:

- Constructs and flies a paper glider according to a set of instructions.
- Uses information to make improvements to a paper glider.

TEACHER INFORMATION:

- Teachers will need to supply A4 sheets of paper, metre rulers and paperclips for the pupils to use.
- Pupils will need a large area like a gymnasium or assembly area (preferably indoors without wind) to practise throwing their gliders.
- Guide pupils step by step to make their own glider.

  * **CAUTION:** Pupils should not throw their gliders at each other.

Fold it down the centre then open it out.	
Fold corners (a) and (b) until they meet the centrefold.	
Now fold corners (c) and (d) until they meet the centrefold.	
Fold the glider upwards along the centrefold. Fold out one wing so (e) meets (f).	
Do the same with the other wing.	
Adjust the wings to the horizontal. Pupils write their names on their gliders.	

ANSWERS:

Teacher check

ADDITIONAL ACTIVITIES TO DEVELOP THIS SKILL:

- Make three different-sized gliders (small, medium and large) and test their performance over several trials. Does size make a difference? Which travels the greatest distance? Have the pupils explain the results.
- Illustrate a set of instructions for making a paper glider.
- From the pupils' findings, have them design and construct their own gliders. Hold a race to see which travels the greatest distance. Examine the winning glider and explain its performance.
- Discuss basic principles of flight and use the information to construct other paper flying machines.

CURRICULUM LINKS

Country	Subject	Level	Objectives
England	Science	KS 2	• Test ideas using evidence from observation and measurement and draw conclusions.
Northern Ireland	Science	KS 2	• Carry out tests, collect data and record results.
Republic of Ireland	Science	3rd/4th Class	• Carry out simple experiments, record data on length and record conclusions.
Scotland	Science	Level C	• Make measurements and observations and record findings.
Wales	Science	KS 2	• Know scientific ideas can be tested by means of information gathered from observation and measurement.

Gliding away ...

> **Task**
> *You will follow a set of instructions to make a paper glider and use information to improve its performance.*

1. Make a paper glider by folding a sheet of A4 paper. Test fly it twice and measure the distance it travels.

Test 1 _________ m _________ cm	**Test 2** _________ m _________ cm

2. Read the information below.

   Try these tips to make your paper glider fly further:

   - Throw it harder.
   - Throw it upwards.
   - Add paperclips to the bottom of the glider.
   - Bend up the wingtips.
   - Add creases to the wings.

   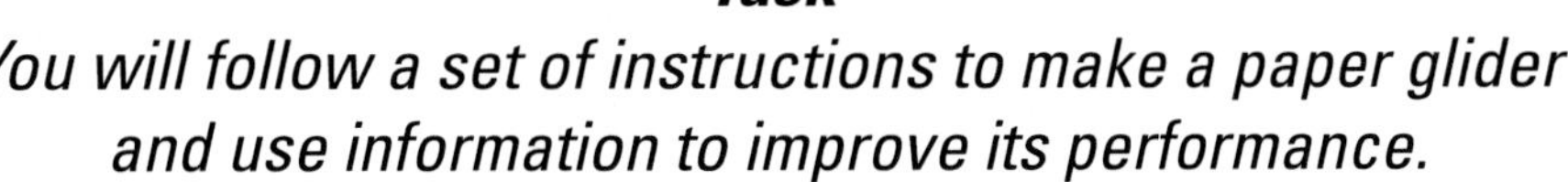

   > Keep any adjustments small or you might make things worse!

3. Circle three of the tips you would like to try. Make the changes to your glider you need to then try two more test flights. Measure the distance of each flight.

Test 1 _________ m _________ cm	**Test 2** _________ m _________ cm

4. Make one more change to try to improve your glider and test fly it again.

   Change: ____

   ____

Test 1 _________ m _________ cm	**Test 2** _________ m _________ cm

5. Write a summary of your overall test flying results.

   ____

   ____

   ____

   ____

THINKING MORE ABOUT THINKING

How did you decide which adjustments to make to your glider? Is there anything else you would have liked to have tried? If you were to do the activity again, what would you do differently?

Teachers notes

APPLYING

> **The skill of applying demonstrates a pupil's ability to use previously learnt material in a new or familiar situation.**

OBJECTIVES:

- Selects natural and built features for an imaginary community.
- Determines the staff and goods and services required by each of the features selected.

TEACHER INFORMATION:

- Communities are groups or categories of people with something in common which distinguishes them in a significant way from other groups. How a community is defined depends on its geographical and cultural boundaries. Generally speaking, a community is a group of people who live in the same area and/or who share some things in common.

ANSWERS:

Teacher check

ADDITIONAL ACTIVITIES TO DEVELOP THIS SKILL:

- Demonstrate how people, services and features of a community relate to each other.
- Compile a list of basic information which should be available in every community.
- Research an unusual community, such as one in an ancient civilisation or a community of scientists living in a biodome or space station.
- Give details about the special requirements of a very sophisticated community, such as that of an advanced alien culture.
- From your knowledge of communities, define common problems which can occur in all communities.
- Using your local community as the example, construct a graphic organiser to show the different components of a community.

CURRICULUM LINKS

Country	Subject	Level	Objectives
England	Geography	KS 2	• Describe what places are like and how they are similar to and different from other places.
Northern Ireland	Geography	KS 2	• Explore how we live and the similarities and differences between places.
Republic of Ireland	Geography	3rd/4th Class	• Be aware of human and natural features in different places.
Scotland	Society	Level B/C	• Describe physical and built features of (local) settlements.
Wales	Geography	KS 2	• Know what different localities are like and how they compare to other places.

Community life

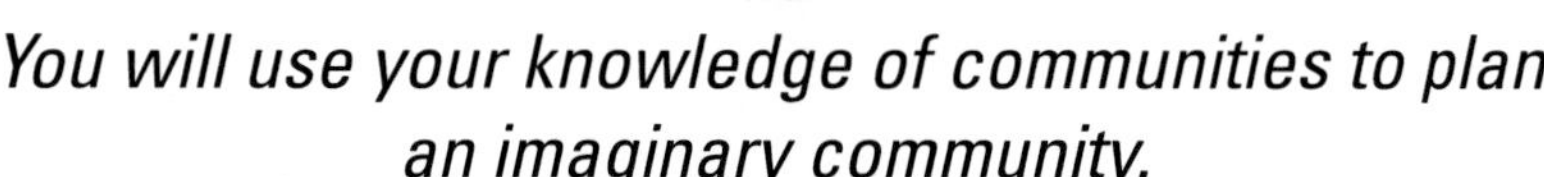

> ***Task***
> *You will use your knowledge of communities to plan*
> *an imaginary community.*

1. Write the name of your imaginary community in the centre then write some of the *built* and *natural* features which could be found there, in each shape. Add extra shapes if needed.

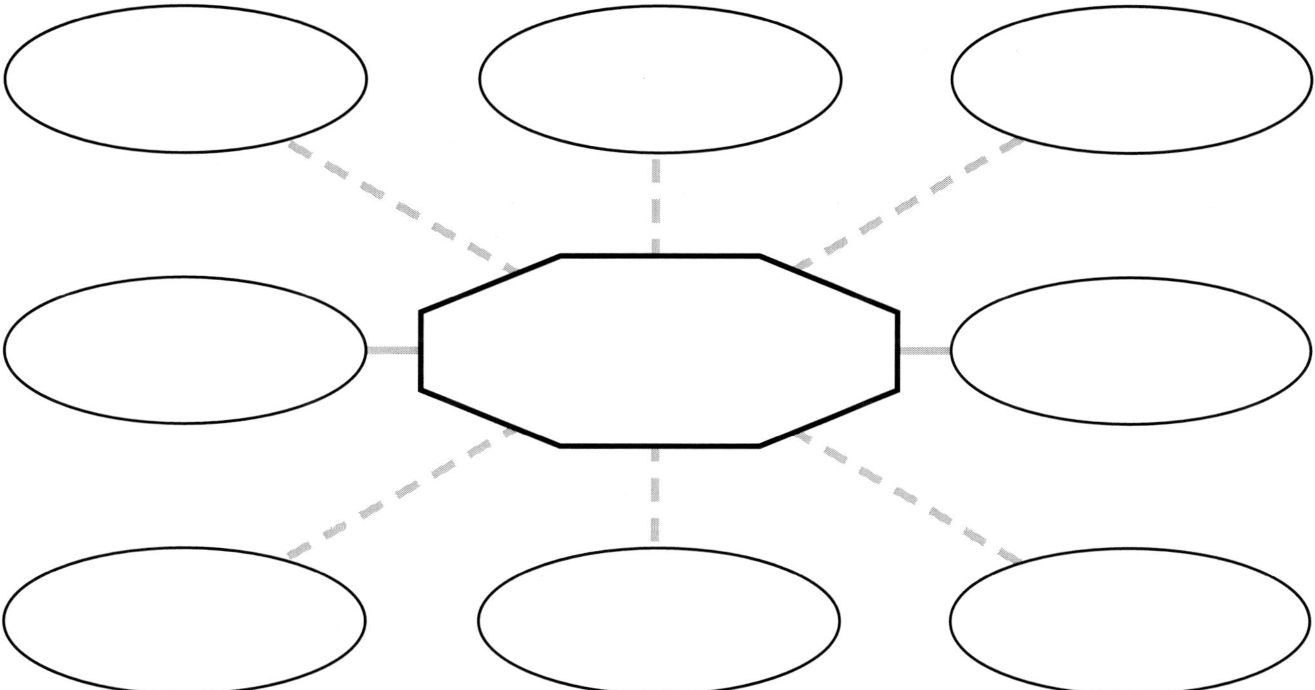

2. In the table below, copy the names of eight features you chose in Question 1. Add the staff and services that would be needed for each feature; for example, a national park would need rangers, a library would need librarians and both could need the services of buses and trains.

Feature	Staff needed	Services

> ***THINKING MORE ABOUT THINKING***
> *Did you include both built and natural features? Why or why not? Could you use this basic information to design a plan or map of your imaginary community? What other features would you need to include other than those listed?*

APPLYING

> The skill of applying demonstrates a pupil's ability to use previously learnt material in a new or familiar situation.

OBJECTIVES:

- Uses knowledge of healthy lifestyle principles to devise a 'kick-start' plan for an unhealthy friend.
- Demonstrates an understanding of difficulties that may be encountered and suggests ideas for support.

TEACHER INFORMATION:

- It is not necessary for pupils to actually have a friend in this situation; it can be hypothetical. It is important, however, that they make realistic suggestions that can be followed and maintained during the course of a normal weekend.
- Allowing pupils to discuss their ideas in small groups before completing the sheet will help them to organise their thoughts.

ANSWERS:

Teacher check

ADDITIONAL ACTIVITIES TO DEVELOP THIS SKILL:

- Prepare a booklet to record information, activities and eating habits, charting progress towards a healthier lifestyle.
- Write a simple recipe booklet for healthy meals and snacks.
- Prepare a talk, using appropriate resources for demonstration, of a chosen sport or physical activity. Include how it helps to promote a healthy lifestyle.

CURRICULUM LINKS

Country	Subject	Level	Objectives
England	PSHE	KS 2	• Know what makes a healthy lifestyle, including the benefits of exercise and healthy eating.
Northern Ireland	PD	KS 2	• Understand the benefits of a healthy lifestyle, including physical activity, healthy eating and rest.
Republic of Ireland	SPHE	3rd/4th Class	• Understand and appreciate what it means to be healthy and to have a balanced lifestyle.
Scotland	Health	Level C	• Show knowledge and understanding of what they need to do to keep healthy; e.g. regular exercise, leisure activities and choosing nutritious food.
Wales	PSE	KS 2	• Understand the benefits of exercise and the need for a variety of food for growth and activity.

Healthy weekend

> ***Task***
> *To devise a healthy weekend plan for a friend who has been living an unhealthy lifestyle.*

For a balanced, healthy lifestyle, we need a variety of foods from the different food groups, as well as regular exercise. Many people do not enjoy such a lifestyle and as a result, are experiencing symptoms of poor health.

1. For the weekend, plan:
   (a) physical activities,
   (b) relaxation activities,
   (c) healthy meals and snacks,

   which your friend will be able to follow and maintain.

	physical activities	*relaxation activities*	*healthy meals and snacks*
Saturday morning			
Saturday afternoon			
Saturday evening			
Sunday morning			
Sunday afternoon			
Sunday evening			

2. (a) Which of your healthy ideas might be the most difficult for your friend? Explain your answer.

   ____

   ____

   (b) How could you support your friend at this time?

   ____

   ____

THINKING MORE ABOUT THINKING
How would your knowledge of a friend affect your choice of plan? What factors would you have to consider for the plan to be continued successfully?

Teachers notes

APPLYING

> The skill of applying demonstrates a pupil's ability to use previously learnt material in a new or familiar situation.

OBJECTIVE:

- Uses sound and music to represent the story of Little Red Riding Hood.

TEACHER INFORMATION:

- The pupils will need to work in groups of four to five for this activity.

- Depending on the level of the pupils, Question 1 could be completed as a class and the main events could be written on the board.

- If appropriate, teachers may like to allow the pupils to choose a different story to dramatise. However, it must be familiar to the pupils, have a simple storyline and contain plenty of scope for including sound and/or music.

- Have a selection of simple materials for the pupils to use to make sound effects; e.g. rice, wood, blocks, various types of paper, drums. Musical instruments can also be used—the pupils could supply their own if this activity is conducted over more than one lesson. Encourage the pupils to also use their voices to create sound effects, although they should not speak.

- After planning and rehearsal time, the pupils can present their productions to the class. Everyone should close their eyes when listening.

ANSWERS:

Teacher check

ADDITIONAL ACTIVITIES TO DEVELOP THIS SKILL:

- Have groups of pupils script and dramatise a range of familiar stories.

- Listen to the musical story 'Peter and the wolf' and have the pupils use the music to help them create their own musical interpretations of the story.

- Have the pupils practise and perform dances to different styles of music.

- Listen to various pieces of music and classify them into different groups; e.g. 'jazz', 'scary', 'slow'.

CURRICULUM LINKS

Country	Subject	Level	Objectives
England	Music	KS 2	• Compose, responding to a range of non-musical starting points.
Northern Ireland	Music	KS 2	• Create stories through sound.
Republic of Ireland	Music	3rd/4th Class	• Select different kinds of sounds to create sound stories.
Scotland	Music	Level C	• Invent sound pictures and develop a sense of structure; e.g. beginning, middle and end.
Wales	Music	KS 2	• Improvise, compose and arrange music in response to extra-musical stimuli.

Story sounds

> **Task**
> *You will use music and sound to tell the story of*
> *Little Red Riding Hood.*

1. Find a small group to work with. Discuss the main events that make up the beginning, middle and end of the fairytale 'Little Red Riding Hood'.

2. Think carefully about how you could use only music and sound to tell the story; for example, playing a 'scary' tune to represent the wolf when he first appears; crunching up paper to represent footsteps on leaves. List the details you decide on in the space below.

3. Practise your performance and then present it to the class.

Beginning	
Event	*Sound/Music*
•	
•	
Middle	
Event	*Sound/Music*
•	
•	
End	
Event	*Sound/Music*
•	
•	

THINKING MORE ABOUT THINKING
How did you choose which sounds would best represent each event? Did you find it easy or difficult to decide on each sound? Did your presentation turn out as you had imagined it?

Thinking challenges 3

Topic focus   **Myth and mystery**

Remembering	• Make a list of mythical beasts you have heard of or read about.
Understanding	• Summarise a favourite myth. • Research to explain why so many people believe the Loch Ness Monster is real.
Applying	• Choose a mythical hero or heroine from a film or book; e.g. Zorro, Hercules, Mulan. If this person was transported forward in time to today, what do you think he/she would be doing?
Analysing	• Write a list of features you think a good mystery novel or story should have.
Evaluating	• Do you believe that every UFO sighting is real? Explain your answer.
Creating	• Write your own myth that explains why something happens in nature; e.g. why spiders spin webs. • In a group, create a radio play with a mystery theme. Use sound effects to add to the tension.

Topic focus   **Flight**

Remembering	• Compile a list of different methods of flight.
Understanding	• Label a simple diagram of a bird's body, showing its adaptations to flight.
Applying	• Make and test fly paper helicopters. • Research to find out interesting facts about bats and flying foxes.
Analysing	• Research to find what you think is the greatest moment in the history of flight. Write reasons for your choice. • Write what you think are the best and worst things about modern jet aircraft travel.
Evaluating	• Comment on the actions of Icarus from the ancient Greek myth about the flight of Icarus. • Write which method of flight you would most like to try. Give reasons.
Creating	• Imagine you are a bird. Describe what it feels like to fly. • Draw and label a futuristic flying machine that will take tourists to the moon.

ANALYSING

ANALYSING: PUPIL SELF-EVALUATION

Use the sections below to record thoughts or information about the worksheets or answers to the metacognitive questions on each pupil page.

Name ____

Pages 52–53   **Comparing characters**

Pages 54–55   **Word problems**

Pages 56–57   **Volcanic eruptions**

Pages 58–59   **Endangered!**

Pages 60–61   **David's health diary**

Pages 62–63   **Feel the rhythm**

ANALYSING

Pages	Title	Key learning areas	Thinking activity
52–53	Comparing characters	English	• Compares himself/herself to a main character from a familiar novel.
54–55	Word problems	Mathematics	• Reads and solves word problems. • Indicates how word problems were solved.
56–57	Volcanic eruptions	Science	• Uses cross-sectional diagrams to complement an explanation of stages of a volcanic eruption. • Highlights subject-specific vocabulary.
58–59	Endangered!	Geography	• Researches specific facts about an endangered animal. • Writes a report about an endangered animal.
60–61	David's health diary	Health	• Reads a diary entry about health issues. • Analyses aspects of a person's lifestyle.
62–63	Feel the rhythm	Dance/Music	• Analyses a piece of music for changes in duration, tempo and texture. • Devises movement to match the mood of the music.

DEFINITION:

The skill of analysing involves exploring the assumptions, ideas or structure inherent in a text or other piece of information. This is done by breaking the information into sections or elements – often visually, through a graphic organiser. Analysing can also help pupils compare the features of two or more texts.

SOME APPROPRIATE VERBS:

compare, attribute, organise, deconstruct, form opinions, make decisions, interpret, infer, deduce, give reasons, analyse, categorise, contrast, separate, calculate, determine, develop, distinguish, estimate, predict, relate, solve, classify etc.

SOME APPROPRIATE GRAPHIC ORGANISERS:

Decision-making Matrix, Disadvantages/Improvements T-chart, Fact/Opinion T-chart, KWL chart, Mind map, PMI, Y chart, 5W chart, Venn diagram, Compare or contrast chart, Compare and contrast chart, Categories tree, Categories pyramid, Chain of events etc.

SOME SUITABLE QUESTIONS:

What are the differences?, Which events could not have happened?, How is this similar to?, What was the idea of … ?, Why did … changes occur?, What was the problem with … ? What might have been the ending if … ?, What other possible solutions do you see?, Can you explain what must have happened when … ?, What was the turning point? etc.

ANALYSING

The skill of analysing involves exploring the assumptions, ideas or structure inherent in a text or other piece of information. This is done by breaking the information into sections or elements—often visually, using a graphic organiser. Analysing can also help pupils compare the features of two or more texts.

OBJECTIVE:

- Compares himself/herself to a main character from a familiar novel.

TEACHER INFORMATION:

- The pupils should choose a main character from a novel they have read recently. This may be a text that has been covered in class or one they have read in their own time.

ANSWERS:

Teacher check

ADDITIONAL ACTIVITIES TO DEVELOP THIS SKILL:

- Hold a formal debate concerning the appropriateness of characters' actions in a familiar novel or story.
- Write critical advice for your character on how he/she should deal with a particular situation.
- Compare your chosen character's best deed with his/her worst deed.
- Consider what might have happened in a character's life to influence him/her to act in a particular way; e.g. commit a crime.

CURRICULUM LINKS

Country	Subject	Level	Objectives
England	English	KS 2	• Find information through scanning and detailed reading.
Northern Ireland	Language and literacy	KS 2	• Use a variety of reading skills, including scanning and consider characters in stories.
Republic of Ireland	English	3rd/4th Class	• Develop basic information retrieval skills, including scanning.
Scotland	English	Level C	• Scan texts for specific information and identify with fictional characters.
Wales	English	KS 2	• Find information through scanning and detailed reading and respond to characters.

Comparing characters

> **Task**
> *You will compare yourself to a character from a novel.*

1. Choose a main character from a novel that you have read and enjoyed. Compare yourself to the character by completing the table below.

	Me	**Character:** _____________
Appearance		
Personality		
Favourite things		
Least favourite things		
Most skilled at …		
Most difficult challenge faced		

2. Mark on the scale how similar you feel you are to this character.

Very similar ⸺⚪⸺⚪⸺⚪⸺⚪⸺⚪⸺ *Very different*

Give reasons for choosing this character. ______________________________

____

____

____

THINKING SKILLS

Teachers notes

ANALYSING

The skill of analysing involves exploring the assumptions, ideas or structure inherent in a text or other piece of information. This is done by breaking the information into sections or elements—often visually, using a graphic organiser. Analysing can also help pupils compare the features of two or more texts.

OBJECTIVES:

- Reads and solves word problems.
- Indicates how word problems were solved.

TEACHER INFORMATION:

- Teachers may wish to survey and graph results to identify pupils experiencing difficulties and any common problems.

ANSWERS:

(a) 284 km + 139 km = 423 km

(b) 12 x 6 = 72 eggs

(c) 24 x 8 = 192 loaves of bread

(d) 578 + 416 = 994 people

(e) 289 – 54 = 235 kg

(f) 15 ÷ 3 = 5 cards

ADDITIONAL ACTIVITIES TO DEVELOP THIS SKILL:

- Pupils create word problems of their own for other pupils to solve.
- Collect, tally and graph survey information about a favourite song or television show and write conclusions.
- Decipher number patterns such as counting backwards from 1000 by 100s, starting at 2 and doubling each number to 128 etc.

CURRICULUM LINKS

Country	Subject	Level	Objectives
England	Maths	KS 2	• Choose and use the four number operations and appropriate ways to calculate to solve word problems involving numbers in 'real life'.
Northern Ireland	Maths and numeracy	KS 2	• Use the four operations to solve problems.
Republic of Ireland	Maths	3rd/4th Class	• Solve word problems involving addition, subtraction, multiplication and division.
Scotland	Maths	Level C	• Add, subtract, multiply and divide in number and measurement.
Wales	Maths	KS 2	• Develop their understanding and use of the four operations to solve problems, including those involving measures, using a calculator where appropriate.

Word problems

> **Task**
> *You will show the processes involved in solving*
> *a word problem.*

1. Read the problem then complete the boxes.

Word problem	Process used: Addition? Subtraction? Multiplication? Division?	Method used: Mental? Written? Calculator?	Answers (including any calculations)
(a) A family drove 284 km on Saturday and 139 km on Sunday. How many kilometres did they travel in total on the weekend?			
(b) Twelve chickens in a henhouse each laid 6 eggs in a week. How many eggs were laid altogether?			
(c) At the supermarket, 8 boxes with 24 loaves of bread in each were delivered. How many loaves of bread were delivered altogether?			
(d) On Saturday, 578 people went to watch the football and 416 people went to watch the cricket. How many people went to watch sport altogether on Saturday?			
(e) The baker had 289 kg of flour. He used 54 kg to bake bread. How much flour does he have left?			
(f) Terry shared his 15 cards among himself and his 2 friends. How many cards did each get?			

THINKING MORE ABOUT THINKING

Which process did you feel more confident to use? Were there any division or multiplication tables involved which you are unsure of and need to practise? Did you use one method to calculate more than another? Or did you use a combination of methods to obtain your answers?

ANALYSING

The skill of analysing involves exploring the assumptions, ideas or structure inherent in a text or other piece of information. This is done by breaking the information into sections or elements—often visually, using a graphic organiser. Analysing can also help pupils compare the features of two or more texts.

OBJECTIVES:

- Uses a cross-sectional diagram to complement an explanation of the stages of a volcanic eruption.
- Highlights subject-specific vocabulary.

TEACHER INFORMATION:

- Discuss the geology of volcanoes. Give pupils access to a range of resources to supplement their current knowledge and understanding of the topic. Encourage pupils to interpret information from the resources and make notes which they will use to complete the activity page.
- Allow pupils to share and discuss their explanations to determine how comprehensive their own work is. They will learn different strategies for developing this skill from their peers.

ANSWERS:

1. Vocabulary should include: magma chamber, magma reservoir, lava, ash, cloud, cone, eruption, gaseous fumes, crucial point, rim
2. Teacher check
3. Answers should include;
   - As gases build up below the earth's surface, liquid rock called magma forms reservoirs in chambers beneath the volcano's crater.
   - As the pressure intensifies, steam and gases from the magma explode into the atmosphere, developing into a thick cloud.
   - Particles of magma also shoot upwards, creating a fountain of fire.
   - The reservoir of magma is forced upwards by the build-up of gaseous pressure and, at the crucial point of the eruption, it escapes by flowing over the rim and oozing through fissures in the side of the volcano's cone.
   - Once the magma has exploded from the volcano, it cascades down the sides of the mountain and is referred to as lava.

ADDITIONAL ACTIVITIES TO DEVELOP THIS SKILL:

- Make a colourful booklet for a younger audience, explaining what happens during a volcanic eruption.
- Find a method, using vinegar and bicarbonate of soda, of making an erupting volcano. Publish the method as a procedure.
- Use a range of materials to make a model of an erupting volcano.

CURRICULUM LINKS

Country	Subject	Level	Objectives
England	Science	KS 2	• Use a range of methods, including diagrams, to communicate information in an appropriate manner.
Northern Ireland	Science	KS 2	• Present information using a range of appropriate ways and use precise subject specific vocabulary.
Republic of Ireland	Science	3rd/4th Class	• Present information using a variety of methods.
Scotland	Science	Level C	• Make a short report, communicating key points clearly and explain using scientific knowledge.
Wales	Science	KS 2	• Use a range of methods, including diagrams, to present information in an appropriate manner and use relevant scientific vocabulary.

Volcanic eruptions

> **Task**
> *You will draw a cross-section of a volcano to explain what happens during an eruption.*

There are about 1500 active volcanoes in the world. They are monitored by *vulcanologists* (volcano experts). They use a range of equipment to predict when a volcano might erupt. These scientists can often warn people living nearby of an impending eruption and so save lives.

1. Write key volcano-related words in the box.

2. Draw a labelled cross-section of a volcano during an eruption.

3. Describe the stages of a volcanic eruption.

____

____

____

____

____

THINKING MORE ABOUT THINKING
How did you organise your information into stages? Have you included all the major stages? How can you check? Could you improve your description?

Teachers notes
ANALYSING

> The skill of analysing involves exploring the assumptions, ideas or structure inherent in a text or other piece of information. This is done by breaking the information into sections or elements—often visually, using a graphic organiser. Analysing can also help pupils compare the features of two or more texts.

OBJECTIVES:

- Researches specific facts about an endangered animal.
- Writes a report about an endangered animal.

TEACHER INFORMATION:

- The pupils will require appropriate reference material to complete the activity.
- When the pupils write their reports, they should use headings or paragraphing to clearly distinguish between each aspect or feature of the animal.

ANSWERS:

Teacher check

ADDITIONAL ACTIVITIES TO DEVELOP THIS SKILL:

- Write the biography of a well-known wildlife conservationist.
- Devise an action plan to help save an endangered animal.
- Compile a questionnaire to find out how much pupils at your school know about endangered animals.
- Comment on what is being done by people to help save endangered animals. Do you think enough is being done?

CURRICULUM LINKS

Country	Subject	Level	Objectives
England	Geography	KS 2	• Use secondary sources of information and recognise how people can improve or damage the environment.
Northern Ireland	Geography	KS 2	• Explore ways people affect the environment and how to best care for a changing environment.
Republic of Ireland	Geography	3rd/4th Class	• Collect and record information from a variety of sources and recognise human activities which may have adverse effects on the environment.
Scotland	Society	Level C	• Select and record specific information and present findings in a report.
Wales	Geography	KS 2	• Use secondary sources for information and investigate ways to safeguard the future environment.

Endangered!

Task
You will research and write a report about an endangered animal.

Hundreds of animal species around the world are under the threat of extinction.

1. Choose one of the endangered animals below or one you already know about. Use the Internet, encyclopedias or other resources to complete the table below and then use it to write a report.

kiwi	*Queen Alexandra's birdwing butterfly*		*koala*
dugong	*green sea turtle*	*snow leopard*	*barn owl*

Name of animal	**Type of animal** mammal .... ☐ reptile .... ☐ bird .... ☐ insect .... ☐ amphibian .... ☐ fish .... ☐
Sketch	**Where does it live?**
Why is it under threat?	**Interesting facts**
What are people doing to try to help it?	
What else do you think should be done?	

2. Write your report on a separate sheet of paper.

THINKING MORE ABOUT THINKING
How did you decide what to put into the interesting facts box? What was the most difficult part of planning your report?

ANALYSING

> The skill of analysing involves exploring the assumptions, ideas or structure inherent in a text or other piece of information. This is done by breaking the information into sections or elements – often visually, using a graphic organiser. Analysing can also help pupils compare the features of two or more texts.

OBJECTIVES:

- Reads a diary entry about health issues.
- Analyses aspects of a person's lifestyle.

TEACHER INFORMATION:

- A healthy, balanced lifestyle should include getting regular exercise, adequate sleep and balancing the demands of work and school with relaxation. More emphasis on one area while neglecting another causes stress, poor health and an inability to cope with the demands of daily life.
- The diary entry given does not allow time for relaxation in an area other than sport. The diet may be inadequate to cater for the amount of exercise done.

ANSWERS:

Teacher check

ADDITIONAL ACTIVITIES TO DEVELOP THIS SKILL:

- Construct a timetable for a more balanced lifestyle for David.
- Compare the daily lifestyles of two classmates and write conclusions about their health.
- Calculate the amount of time spent on exercise, school work, chores and relaxation in an average day.
- Draw diagrams or graphs to illustrate the balance between exercise, sleep, relaxation and diet.
- Hold a debate on the topic 'There is no such thing as too much exercise' OR ' It's okay to eat a lot of junk food as long as you get a lot of exercise'.

CURRICULUM LINKS

Country	Subject	Level	Objectives
England	PSHE	KS 2	• Know what makes a healthy lifestyle, including the benefits of exercise and healthy eating.
Northern Ireland	PD	KS 2	• Understand the benefits of a healthy lifestyle, including physical activity, healthy eating and rest.
Republic of Ireland	SPHE	3rd/4th Class	• Understand and appreciate what it means to be healthy and to have a balanced lifestyle.
Scotland	Health	Level C	• Show knowledge and understanding of what they need to do to keep healthy; e.g. regular exercise, leisure activities and choosing nutritious food.
Wales	PSE	KS 2	• Understand the benefits of exercise and the need for a variety of food for growth and activity.

David's health diary

Task

You will read and analyse a diary entry about health issues.

1. Read the diary entry below.

Monday 3 April

Woke at 6 am for swimming training. Guzzled a glass of orange juice before Mum shuffled me into the car. Pushed myself hard this morning as the coach was really grumpy. Achieved a better time though!

Home at 7.30 am for a shower and breakfast. Ran to catch the bus at 8.15 am.

Handed in my reading assignment but was not happy with it because I knew I could have done a better job of it.

Won the maths mentals game for my team today, but since I love doing maths no-one was really surprised.

Played a really tough game of football at lunchtime and helped Josh to finish his crisps and cola.

Wrote about our footy game for writing and the teacher seemed pleased. Started my mapping project with Shane. Wish he'd help out more though. I seem to be doing all the research while he draws pretty pictures.

Left half of my salad roll to play football. Didn't play as well as I would have liked! Ate an apple on the way to cricket practice. Tea, homework and bed. Each day sure seems to fly!

---

2. Use the table to analyse aspects of the way David looks after his health.

What positive things does David do to be healthy?	What negative things does David do which could cause problems?	What aspects of being healthy does David not include?

THINKING MORE ABOUT THINKING

Did you identify everything you could have? Did you find it easy or hard to think of other healthy things for David to include? Did you need to read the diary entry again to make sure that you had included everything for each column?

ANALYSING

The skill of analysing involves exploring the assumptions, ideas or structure inherent in a text or other piece of information. This is done by breaking the information into sections or elements—often visually, using a graphic organiser. Analysing can also help pupils compare the features of two or more texts.

OBJECTIVES:

- Analyses a piece of music for changes in duration, tempo and texture.
- Devises movement to match the mood of the music.

TEACHER INFORMATION:

- Pupils will need prior experience and knowledge of some of the elements of music—e.g. (duration, pitch, texture, timbre, dynamics, tempo and form)—and dance—e.g. (body, energy, space and time).
- While pupils work in groups to choose and discuss the music and movements, they should be allowed to choose their exact movement and perform independently within the group if they wish.
- Pupils will begin to see how a composer puts the different elements of music together and their understanding of this will be highlighted by how their dancing flows as the music changes.

ANSWERS:

Teacher check

ADDITIONAL ACTIVITIES TO DEVELOP THIS SKILL:

- Listen to two very different and two very similar pieces of music and note the changes over time within each. Compare the similarities and differences between each pair.
- Choose a familiar, favourite piece of music. Weave a short story or poem through it. Add movement to match the story and the music.
- Use stick man sketches to illustrate movement to a piece of music. Display the sketches on a white background with a black border. Include the title of the music, printed in black ink.

CURRICULUM LINKS

Country	Subject	Level	Objectives
England	PE	KS 2	• Create and perform dances in response to a range of stimuli and accompaniment.
Northern Ireland	PE	KS 2	• Respond through dance to a variety of stimuli; e.g. music.
Republic of Ireland	PE	3rd/4th Class	• Respond through dance to stimuli such as music.
Scotland	PE	Level C	• Structure ideas for the start, middle and end of a dance.
Wales	PE	KS 2	• Respond imaginatively to different stimuli and put forward their ideas about what to include in a simple dance.

Feel the rhythm

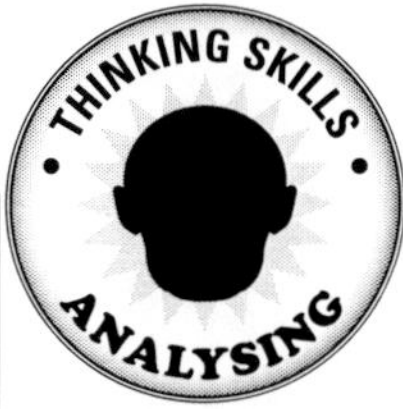

Task

You will choreograph a dance in response to a piece of music.

When listening to music, people often like to move with the rhythm, even if it is only a little foot tapping. Different music gives us different ideas for ways to move. Dancing is a natural and fulfilling experience which many of us enjoy.

1. (a) In a small group, choose a piece of familiar music (about five minutes long) to choreograph. It may be a song or an instrumental piece.

   (b) Listen carefully to the music and note how it changes in tempo and texture. Record these changes in the table below.

   (c) Discuss how you will make the dance match the changes in the mood of the music. Write adverbs and phrases to describe how you will move.

Title of music/song:		
time (min.)	**changes**	**movement**

2. Perform your dance for the rest of the class.

Thinking challenges 4

<table>
<tr><td>Topic focus</td><td colspan="2">Climate and weather</td></tr>
<tr><td>Remembering</td><td colspan="2">• Make a number of illustrated cards for the types of weather experienced throughout the world.
• Make a list of instruments meteorologists use to record the weather.</td></tr>
<tr><td>Understanding</td><td colspan="2">• On four maps of your country, pin weather cards to indicate typical weather around the country for each season.</td></tr>
<tr><td>Applying</td><td colspan="2">• Design weather charts to be included in a holiday brochure for each season in your country.</td></tr>
<tr><td>Analysing</td><td colspan="2">• Choose one weather pattern and explain, using a labelled diagram, how it occurs and how it is affected by the physical features of the landscape.
• Make a model of an instrument used by meteorologists. Explain what it is used for and how it works.</td></tr>
<tr><td>Evaluating</td><td colspan="2">• Complete a table recording the similarities and differences of the climate regions of Europe.</td></tr>
<tr><td>Creating</td><td colspan="2">• Write an article for a magazine, highlighting the positive aspects of living in each climate region of Europe.
• Design a poster, illustrating the different weather-related outdoor activities we can participate in.</td></tr>
</table>

<table>
<tr><td>Topic focus</td><td colspan="2">Food chains</td></tr>
<tr><td>Remembering</td><td colspan="2">• Write a simple explanation, with diagrams, of a food chain.
• Design posters illustrating food chains in different environments.</td></tr>
<tr><td>Understanding</td><td colspan="2">• On a Venn diagram, glue pictures of carnivores, herbivores and omnivores.
• Make a booklet with three pages headed, 'producers', 'consumers' and 'decomposers'. Collect pictures to glue on each page.</td></tr>
<tr><td>Applying</td><td colspan="2">• Draw and illustrate a food chain for animals living on the African savanna.
• Write and perform a simple play for a younger audience, explaining the idea of a food chain.</td></tr>
<tr><td>Analysing</td><td colspan="2">• Choose one animal from a food chain, and explain how it captures its prey and hides from its predators.</td></tr>
<tr><td>Evaluating</td><td colspan="2">• Draw diagrams to describe the difference between examples of a food chain and a food web.
• Explain the consequences of removing one link from a food chain.</td></tr>
<tr><td>Creating</td><td colspan="2">• Using texture, colour and form, create a display of a marine food chain.
• Compose a music and movement score to accompany a poem about plants and animals in a food chain.
• Devise an outdoor game called 'Climbing the food chain'.</td></tr>
</table>

EVALUATING

Use the sections below to record thoughts or information about the worksheets or answers to the metacognitive questions on each pupil page.

Name ....

Pages 68–69	**In my opinion**

Pages 70–71	**Golden prize problem**

Pages 72–73	**Rubber chicken bones**

Pages 74–75	**Map-making challenge**

Pages 76–77	**A balanced life**

Pages 78–79	**Be an art critic!**

Teacher introduction
EVALUATING

Pages	Title	Key learning areas	Thinking activity
68–69	In my opinion	English	• Selects favourite book and character from the book and explains their appeal.
70–71	Golden prize problem	Mathematics	• Decides on the best method for solving a word problem. • Compares his/her method of solving a word problem with that of others.
72–73	Rubber chicken bones	Science	• Reads and follows instructions to conduct an experiment. • Evaluates an experiment.
74–75	Map-making challenge	Geography	• Chooses appropriate symbols for each feature on the map. • Determines the best position for each feature based on knowledge of human activity and how it interacts with the environment.
76–77	A balanced life	Health	• Reflects on which areas of his/her life need improvement. • Suggests some ways he/she could improve areas of his/her life.
78–79	Be an art critic!	Art	• Selects and writes evaluations of his/her artwork.

DEFINITION:

The skill of evaluating involves judging the merits of ideas according to a set of criteria, standards or values. Evaluating may require pupils to reflect on or criticise information or justify a decision or course of action.

SOME APPROPRIATE VERBS:

assess, decide, measure, select, conclude, compare, summarise, judge, recommend, critique, justify, check, evaluate, choose, rate, revise, score, validate, value, test, argue, prioritise, verify etc.

SOME APPROPRIATE GRAPHIC ORGANISERS:

Advantages/Disadvantages T-chart, Decision-making matrix, PMI chart, Relevant/Irrelevant T-chart, Y-chart, Fact/Opinion T-chart, 5Ws diagram, Continuum, Problem/Solution organiser etc.

SOME SUITABLE QUESTIONS:

Is there a better solution to … ?, Do you think … is a good or bad thing?, What changes would you recommend to … ?, How would you feel if … ?, How effective is … ?, What do you think about …?, Do you believe … ?, How would you have … ? etc.

Teachers notes

Evaluating

> **The skill of evaluating involves judging the merits of ideas according to a set of criteria, standards or values.**

OBJECTIVE:

- Selects favourite book and character from the book and explains their appeal.

TEACHER INFORMATION:

- Discuss pupils' favourite narrative genres. Revise the standard format of a narrative: orientation, complication and events, conclusion. Explain how a good author weaves the plot through each section, tying up all loose ends, and uses descriptive language to help the reader become a part of the story.

- Allow pupils to discuss, in small groups, their proposed answers before completing the activity. Suggest that their answers should be inspiring enough to convince someone to read their choice of book.

ANSWERS:

Teacher check

ADDITIONAL ACTIVITIES TO DEVELOP THIS SKILL:

- Compile a list of favourite books. For each book, write one sentence that sums up why it is on your list.

- Write a list of things you believe make a book an enjoyable read. Use this list to rank your favourite books.

- Choose a successful author who has written a number of popular books. Why do you think these books are so popular?

CURRICULUM LINKS

Country	Subject	Level	Objectives
England	English	KS 2	• Read a range of literature and express preferences.
Northern Ireland	Language and literacy	KS 2	• Explore familiar stories, focus on distinctive features; e.g. characters and develop their own preferences.
Republic of Ireland	English	3rd/4th Class	• Talk about choice of books and different reading tastes, the reasons for choices and characters.
Scotland	English	Level C	• Read fiction and identify with characters.
Wales	English	KS 2	• Read a wide range of literature and respond to characters.

In my opinion

Task

To explain reasons for your choice of favourite book and favourite character in the book.

As individuals, we have our own opinions about the best fiction books to read and our favourite characters in those books. No-one can tell us we are wrong in our choices, but they may wonder why we make them.

1. (a) Choose a favourite book.

   (b) Complete the table, giving as much information as you can.

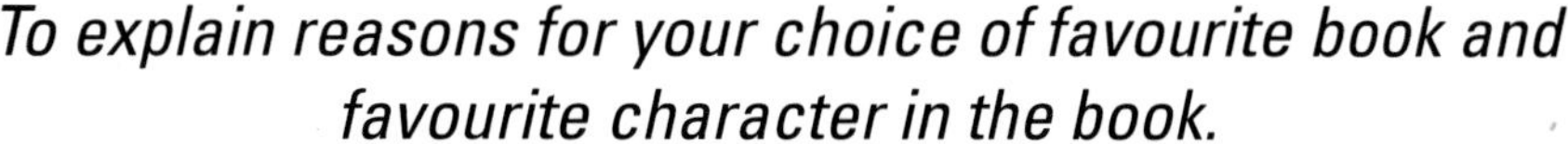

Book title and author:	Genre:

What about this genre appeals to you?

Explain the plot and why it appeals to you.

Who is your favourite character?

What role does he/she play?

Describe him/her (looks, personality, character type).

Why do you like this character? Give examples of some of the things he/she does.

Evaluating

The skill of evaluating involves judging the merits of ideas according to a set of criteria, standards or values.

OBJECTIVES:

- Decides on the best method for solving a word problem.
- Compares his/her method of solving a word problem with that of others.

TEACHER INFORMATION:

- Once the pupils have found partners, teachers should read the word problem and make sure the pupils understand the pattern involved—perhaps by discussing what prizes would be received on Day 5.
- Pupils can use any methods they like to solve the problems, including addition and multiplication. Calculators may be used, but this will produce less variation in methods.
- For Question 3 (b), teachers may like to present two or more different methods for solving the problem to discuss with the class, instead of the pupils comparing their methods with other pairs.

ANSWERS:

2. (a)   bracelets and pendants (20 of each)

   (b)   120

3. Teacher check

ADDITIONAL ACTIVITIES TO DEVELOP THIS SKILL:

- Introduce different methods of multiplication to the pupils; e.g. Napier's bones. How do they feel this compares to the way they are taught to multiply at school?
- Compare codes that use numbers, giving reasons why they are easy or difficult to use.
- Suggest improvements to our system of writing numbers.

CURRICULUM LINKS

Country	Subject	Level	Objectives
England	Maths	KS 2	• Choose and use the four number operations and appropriate ways to calculate to solve word problems involving numbers in 'real life' and explain their methods.
Northern Ireland	Maths and numeracy	KS 2	• Use the four operations to solve problems.
Republic of Ireland	Maths	3rd/4th Class	• Solve word problems involving addition, subtraction, multiplication and division.
Scotland	Maths	Level C	• Add, subtract, multiply and divide in number.
Wales	Maths	KS 2	• Develop their understanding and use of the four operations to solve problems, using a calculator where appropriate and record their methods.

Golden prize problem

Task

You will solve a word problem and then reflect on how you did it.

1. Find a partner to work with. Imagine that you enter a competition together. Three weeks later, you receive the following letter:

Congratulations!

You have won our competition! Your solid gold prizes will be delivered over the next eight days, following this pattern:

Day 1 – 1 pen. **Day 2** – 2 bangles, 1 pen. **Day 3** – 3 clocks, 2 bangles, 1 pen.

This will continue until Day 8, when you will receive 8 necklaces, 7 rings, 6 watches, 5 pendants, 4 bracelets, 3 clocks, 2 bangles and 1 pen.

---

2. Which prize(s) will you receive the most of? How many prizes will you receive altogether? With your partner, decide on the best way to solve these problems. Show any working in the space below.

(a) The prize(s) we will receive the most of is/are: _________________.

(b) Altogether, we will receive _________________ prizes.

3. (a) What were the best and worst things about the way you solved the problems?

Best	Worst

(b) Find another pair who solved the problems in a different way. Which do you think is better?

☐ Ours ☐ Theirs

Give a reason. _________________

THINKING MORE ABOUT THINKING
How did you decide on the best way to solve the problems? How difficult do you normally find it to decide on things? What helps you to make decisions?

Evaluating

> The skill of evaluating involves judging the merits of ideas according to a set of criteria, standards or values.

OBJECTIVES:

- Reads and follows instructions to conduct an experiment.
- Evaluates an experiment.

TEACHER INFORMATION:

- Vinegar, although a mild acid, is strong enough to dissolve the calcium in the bone. Once the calcium is dissolved, there is nothing to keep the bone hard. Only soft bone tissue is left. Consequently, the bone should become more flexible and bend.

ANSWERS:

Teacher check

ADDITIONAL ACTIVITIES TO DEVELOP THIS SKILL:

- Rate the experiment in terms of the ease of being able to obtain the materials, the ease of completion of the task, the degree of success and the amount of interest shown by pupils in completing the experiment.
- Pupils judge how valuable the experiment was for learning new information or to reinforce a procedure for an experiment.
- Conduct the experiment with a partner and evaluate how well you worked together.
- Pupils recommend a similar experiment which aims to change the make-up of foodstuffs.
- Pupils write conclusions for the experiment.
- Revise the experiment using a different liquid in the jar and write conclusions.

CURRICULUM LINKS

Country	Subject	Level	Objectives
England	Science	KS 2	• Make a fair test.
Northern Ireland	Science	KS 2	• Carry out fair tests.
Republic of Ireland	Science	3rd/4th Class	• Carry out simple investigations.
Scotland	Science	Level B	• Use simple equipment to make observations.
Wales	Science	KS 2	• Carry out fair tests.

Rubber chicken bones

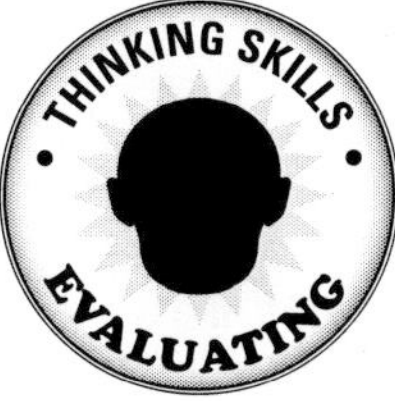

> **Task**
> *You will follow a procedure to conduct an experiment,
> then evaluate its success.*

1. Read the procedure and conduct the experiment.

Aim: *To find out if chicken bones can be changed.*

Materials: Collect the following materials:

~ a jar

~ a chicken bone (leg or drumstick bones work best)

~ vinegar

Method: (a) Rinse the bone in water to remove any remaining meat.

(b) Test the bone by trying to bend it. (It should feel hard.)

(c) Put the bone into the jar and pour in vinegar until the bone is covered.

(d) Remove the bone after three days.

(e) Rinse and try to bend it.

2. Complete the answers to evaluate your experiment.

(a) Was your experiment successful? 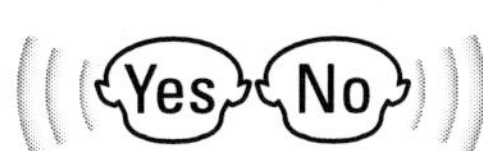

(b) State why it was successful or not.

____

____

____

____

(c) Did you enjoy conducting this simple experiment? 

(d) State why or why not.

____

____

____

THINKING MORE ABOUT THINKING
*Were you able to predict the outcome of the experiment before it was carried out? Were you familiar enough
with a procedure for an experiment that you could easily follow one? Did you make any mistakes following
the experiment which may have caused it to be unsuccessful?*

Teachers notes

Evaluating

> **The skill of evaluating involves judging the merits of ideas according to a set of criteria, standards or values.**

OBJECTIVES:

- Chooses appropriate symbols for each feature on the map.
- Determines the best position for each feature based on knowledge of human activity and how it interacts with the environment.

TEACHER INFORMATION:

- When choosing symbols for the key, pupils should consider easy-to-repeat symbols that clearly represent each feature.
- Pupils need to consider the most appropriate location for each feature, based on their knowledge of human interaction with the environment. Suggest that each time they make a decision, they ask themselves, 'Why?'
- When pupils have positioned all features listed, they may add others, provided they can justify their inclusion.

ANSWERS:

Teacher check

ADDITIONAL ACTIVITIES TO DEVELOP THIS SKILL:

- Study a large-scale, detailed map of a small town which includes some natural features. In one colour, highlight and list the natural features. Repeat for major built features using another colour. Discuss reasons for the location of the built features, with respect to the natural features.
- Study two maps of your country of the same scale, one of the natural (physical) features, the other showing built features; e.g. towns, cities, transport routes. Discuss reasons for the location of the built features, with respect to the natural features.
- Conduct a debate about the destruction of a natural feature to make way for a built feature.

CURRICULUM LINKS

Country	Subject	Level	Objectives
England	Geography	KS 2	• Draw plans and maps.
Northern Ireland	Geography	KS 2	• Use maps.
Republic of Ireland	Geography	3rd/4th Class	• Make simple maps and use common map features; e.g. symbols, key.
Scotland	Society	Level C	• Use maps.
Wales	Geography	KS 2	• Make maps and plans, including keys.

Map-making challenge

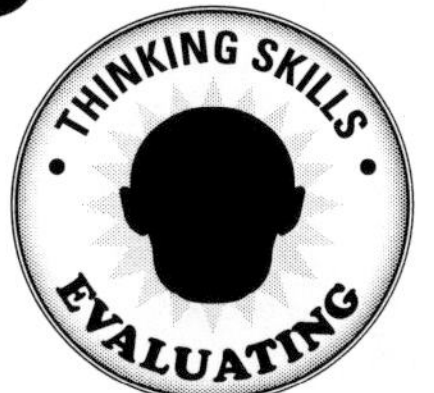

> **Task**
>
> *You will make a map of an imaginary place, giving thought to the position of each feature.*

Maps are plans of an area as seen from a 'bird's eye'. Each map has a scale so the actual distance covered by the map on the ground can be calculated.

1. Design a symbol for each feature in the key.

feature	symbol	feature	symbol	feature	symbol
forest		railway station		emergency services	
hill		railway line		medical centre	
river		bus station		shopping centre	
beach		bus stop		sports centre	
road		taxi rank		house	

2. On a separate sheet of paper, design your map, then copy it in the space below.

3. (a) On a separate sheet of paper, make brief notes to explain why you have positioned the features as you have.

   (b) In a small group, discuss your maps.

THINKING MORE ABOUT THINKING
What did you have in mind when designing your map? What changes might improve the map? Why would you make these changes? If your imaginary place existed, would it be considered well-planned?

Teachers notes

Evaluating

> The skill of evaluating involves judging the merits of ideas according to a set of criteria, standards or values.

OBJECTIVES:

- Reflects on which areas of his/her life need improvement.
- Suggests some ways he/she could improve areas of his/her life.

TEACHER INFORMATION:

- Teachers should make sure the pupils understand that their answers to Question 2 should reflect the sentences they ticked in Question 1.

ANSWERS:

Teacher check

ADDITIONAL ACTIVITIES TO DEVELOP THIS SKILL:

- Have the pupils keep a record of all the changes they made and write how they feel at the end of a given period after implementing them.
- Imagine yourself living the most unhealthy life possible. What do you think might happen to you?
- Read about the daily life of a professional athlete. Decide whether or not this lifestyle would be for you.

CURRICULUM LINKS

Country	Subject	Level	Objectives
England	PSHE	KS 2	• Know what makes a healthy lifestyle, including the benefits of exercise and healthy eating.
Northern Ireland	PD	KS 2	• Understand the benefits of a healthy lifestyle, including physical activity, healthy eating and rest.
Republic of Ireland	SPHE	3rd/4th Class	• Understand and appreciate what it means to be healthy and to have a balanced lifestyle.
Scotland	Health	Level C	• Show knowledge and understanding of what they need to do to keep healthy; e.g. regular exercise, leisure activities and choosing nutritious food.
Wales	PSE	KS 2	• Understand the benefits of exercise and the need for a variety of food for growth and activity.

A balanced life

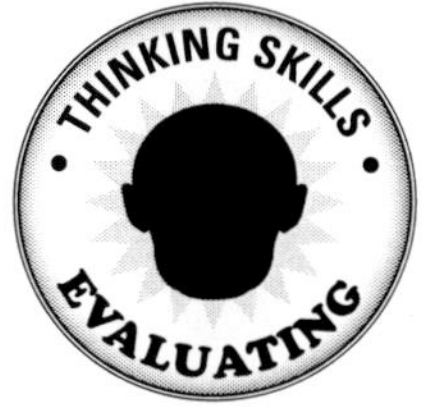

> ***Task***
> *You will suggest some ways to improve your lifestyle.*

A person who has a balanced life tries to eat healthy food, gets regular exercise, enjoys some relaxation as well as work and gets enough sleep to cope with the demands of daily life.

1. Tick the sentences which best describe aspects of your life.

    (a) *My diet is reasonably healthy.* .... ☐

    (b) *My diet needs improvement.* .... ☐

    (c) *I get enough exercise each week.* .... ☐

    (d) *I need to exercise more each week.* .... ☐

    (e) *I spend a lot of time doing things that are not very active.* .... ☐

    (f) *I spend two hours or less each day on sedentary (non-moving) activities.* .... ☐

    (g) *I spend too much time on school work each day.* .... ☐

    (h) *I have interests which help me to relax.* .... ☐

    (i) *I get enough sleep each night.* .... ☐

2. Referring to the sentences above, suggest some ways you can improve your life to provide more balance.

Diet	Sleep	Exercise
Relaxation	School work	

3. Circle one of the above suggestions to try for a week. At the end of the week, decide if you feel better or not and why. Write your comments below.

____

____

____

Teachers notes

Evaluating

> **The skill of evaluating involves judging the merits of ideas according to a set of criteria, standards or values.**

OBJECTIVE:

- Selects and writes evaluations of his/her own artwork.

TEACHER INFORMATION:

- Critiquing their own work encourages pupils to make improvements and develop as artists. During this process pupils should identify what is good and what is bad about their finished products. This may encourage them to identify and concentrate on improving one aspect of their work at a time.

- Pupils may develop their own criteria for evaluating their artworks.

ANSWERS:

Teacher check

ADDITIONAL ACTIVITIES TO DEVELOP THIS SKILL:

- Pupils construct a table, questionnaire or chart which may be used each time they complete an artwork. Compare with previous artworks to assess development.

- Write an evaluation of an artwork of a well-known artist after an excursion to an art gallery or by using resources from the library or Internet.

- Pupils may wish to locate and recommend a particular artwork by a well-known artist which displays features included in their own (or others') work.

- Pupils justify why they would like to change different aspects of their own artwork.

CURRICULUM LINKS

Country	Subject	Level	Objectives
England	Art and design	KS 2	• Evaluate their work and say what they think and feel about it.
Northern Ireland	Art and design	KS 2	• Evaluate their own and others' work.
Republic of Ireland	Visual arts	3rd/4th Class	• Look at and talk about his/her work.
Scotland	Art and design	Level D	• Evaluate their own and others' work.
Wales	Art	KS 2	• Describe and make comparisons between their own work and that of others.

Be an art critic!

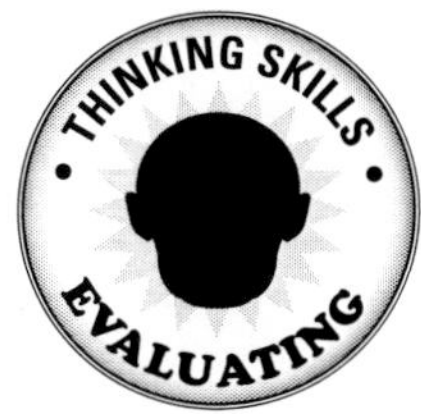

Task
You will evaluate a piece of your own artwork.

1. Select an artwork you have recently completed. You may choose a drawing, 3-D construction, piece of pottery or a painting.

   What piece of art have you chosen and why?

   I have chosen ____

   because ____

   ____.

2. Use the headings below to write an objective evaluation of your artwork.

(a) **Ideas:**	**Your opinion**
• Was the idea for your artwork a good one? Did it work out as you had planned? • Were you able to use personal experiences to develop your ideas? • Were you able to complete the artwork within the time given? • Does your artwork convey the message, idea or image that you wanted?	
(b) **Skills and processes:** • Did you choose the right skills or techniques to suit the subject of your artwork? • Did the lines, colours, textures and shapes suit your image? • Were other class members able to understand and appreciate your artwork?	**Your opinion** *(what was good and what was bad)*

THINKING MORE ABOUT THINKING

How could evaluating your own work help to develop your skills as an artist? Were you more critical of your own work than you should have been? Did you find some good things about your own artwork?

Thinking challenges 5

Remembering	• Identify five inventions which have resulted in enormous changes to daily life.
Understanding	• Explain simply how these inventions work. • Describe what impact these inventions have had on industrial development, for making life easier in households or workplaces, or leading to further development or change.
Applying	• Show how life would be different if each of these inventions had not happened.
Analysing	• Compare the original inventions with the modern-day versions. • Compare the impact of two different inventions.
Evaluating	• Summarise one or two problems (such as pollution) which may have arisen due to each of these inventions.
Creating	• Plan and design an invention of your own which you feel would make your life more interesting or easier.

Topic focus   **Devastating disasters**

Remembering	• Write details of a disaster you have read about recently in a newspaper or magazine.
Understanding	• On a map of the world, locate the place where this disaster took place. • Use diagrams to explain how the disaster occurred.
Applying	• Show how this disaster affected the people who lived in the area. • Give examples of how neighbouring countries or cities assisted the people affected by the disaster.
Analysing	• Compare this disaster to a similar one which occurred in another place at another time.
Evaluating	• Assess the effectiveness of emergency services in dealing with the disaster.
Creating	• Devise an early warning system which could be used to warn disaster-prone areas of disaster. • Create an emergency procedure poster for dealing with the disaster.

CREATING

Pupil checklist

CREATING: PUPIL SELF-EVALUATION

Use the sections below to record thoughts or information about the worksheets or answers to the metacognitive questions on each pupil page.

Name ....

Pages 84–85 **Bear Mountain**

Pages 86–87 **Landscape gardener**

Pages 88–89 **Superbird**

Pages 90–91 **A new enterprise**

Pages 92–93 **Track and field**

Pages 94–95 **Magazine characters**

Teacher introduction
CREATING

Pages	Title	Key learning areas	Thinking activity
84–85	Bear Mountain	English	• Uses a graphic organiser to plan a legend.
86–87	Landscape gardener	Maths/Geography	• Draws a scaled plan of a garden with chosen features. • Explains choice and position of features.
88–89	Superbird	Science	• Draws and labels an imaginary bird that is perfectly adapted to a particular habitat.
90–91	A new enterprise	Geography	• Completes information about a proposed retail enterprise. • Designs and draws aspects of a proposed retail enterprise.
92–93	Track and field	PE	• Devises original track and field events. • Records equipment required and gives a brief description of each event.
94–95	Magazine characters	Drama	• Creates a character from a magazine picture. • Performs a drama scene using a created character.

DEFINITION:

The skill of creating involves using previous knowledge to produce new ideas and different ways of seeing things. Generating new ways to deliver and show understanding of a concept may involve multiple intelligences.

SOME APPROPRIATE VERBS:

arrange, rearrange, combine, create, design, invent, hypothesise, develop, plan, produce, construct, extend ideas, give alternative … , assemble, compose, formulate, modify, propose, predict, devise etc.

SOME APPROPRIATE GRAPHIC ORGANISERS:

Disadvantages/Improvements T-chart, Y-chart, Cloud/Cluster, Concept map, Mind map, Word web etc.

SOME SUITABLE QUESTIONS:

Can you design … ?, How many ways can you … ?, Can you develop … ?, Devise your own ways to … , What would happen if … ?, Can you create new uses for … ? etc.

Teachers notes

Creating

> The skill of creating involves using previous knowledge to produce new ideas and different ways of seeing things.

OBJECTIVE:

- Uses a graphic organiser to plan a legend.

TEACHER INFORMATION:

- Pupils should be familiar with the following information about narratives before commencing this activity:
  - ~ Narratives must have a title which is appropriate and interesting.
  - ~ An orientation introduces the characters and gives information about the characters, where the story happened and the time the story took place.
  - ~ Narratives have a complication involving the main character.
  - ~ A sequence of events is described.
  - ~ A logical, believable resolution to the complication is presented.
  - ~ The narrative has a satisfactory conclusion.
- Writing legends enables pupils to be creative within a familiar format and to explain the reasons for natural formations existing.
- Story maps are a useful tool to enable pupils to plan a story by isolating the various elements needed. Story maps may summarise the beginning, middle and end of a story; list the 5 Ws (who, when, where, what and why); list a complex chain of events summarising all the key elements of a story in chronological order; or may be a pictorial representation of the major events in chronological order.

ANSWERS:

Teacher check

ADDITIONAL ACTIVITIES TO DEVELOP THIS SKILL:

- Pupils select a different type of story to plan for their legends.
- Pupils create a pictorial representation of the main events of a legend.
- Pupils may work with a partner to formulate plans for other legends.
- Pupils compose a short script to explain the formation or existence of Bear Mountain.

CURRICULUM LINKS

Country	Subject	Level	Objectives
England	English	KS 2	• Plan and write using a range of forms.
Northern Ireland	Language and literacy	KS 2	• Plan and write creatively using a variety of forms.
Republic of Ireland	English	3rd/4th Class	• Write stories that explore a variety of genres.
Scotland	English	Level C	• Develop imaginative writing.
Wales	English	KS 2	• Plan and write using imaginative forms.

THINKING SKILLS   www.prim-ed.com • Prim-Ed Publishing

Bear Mountain

Task

You will plan an outline of a legend which explains how a family of bears became a famous mountain.

Use the graphic organiser to plan your story.

Title

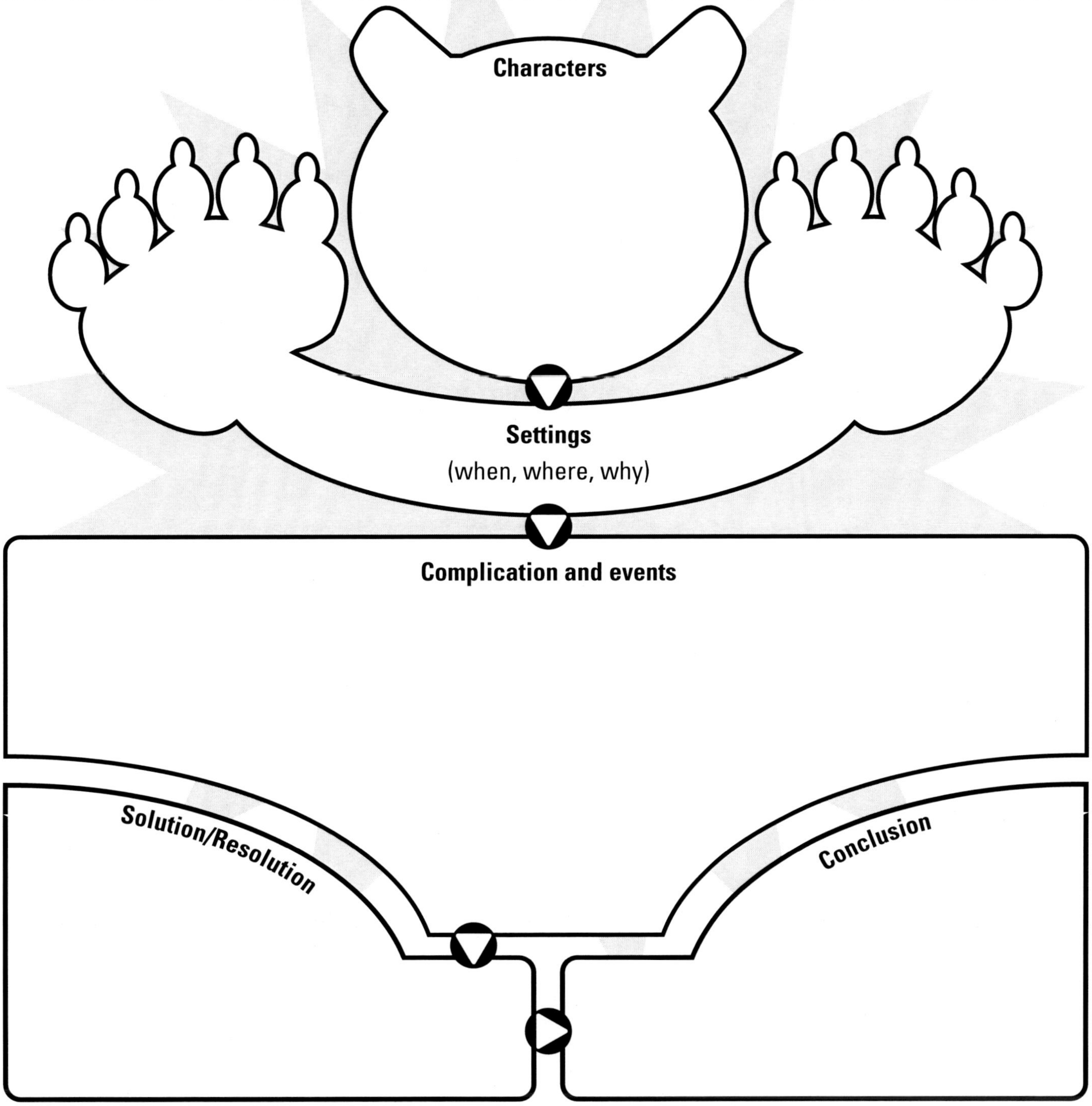

Characters

Settings
(when, where, why)

Complication and events

Solution/Resolution

Conclusion

Teachers notes

Creating

> **The skill of creating involves using previous knowledge to produce new ideas and different ways of seeing things.**

OBJECTIVES:

- Draws a scaled plan of a garden with chosen features.
- Explains choice and position of features.

TEACHER INFORMATION:

- Discuss the value of gardens for pupils and their families. Consider different features which maximise the pleasure and practical purposes of gardens. Highlight the differences in size of gardens and discuss the advantages and disadvantages of large and small plots.
- Depending on the pupils' ability and previous knowledge, discuss specific requirements of sunshine and shade and how this will determine the position of certain features.
- Take pupils outside to measure the actual area of the garden they want to landscape and to decide areas for each feature. (For practical purposes, set a maximum area.) Back inside, allow pupils to make a scale model of their gardens, using blocks and other resources to represent each feature.
- Pupils use the 1cm² grid paper to make scaled drawings of their gardens.

ANSWERS:

Teacher check

ADDITIONAL ACTIVITIES TO DEVELOP THIS SKILL:

- Produce a promotional booklet for an imaginary large garden which is open to the public and boasts, 'Something to delight the whole family!'
- Sketch a line drawing of a new plant you have engineered by cross-pollinating two existing plants.
- Make a collection of pictures of native plants and make up new names for each based on their appearance.

CURRICULUM LINKS

Country	Subject	Level	Objectives
England	Geography	KS 2	• Draw maps and plans at a range of scales.
Northern Ireland	Maths and numeracy	KS 2	• Understand and use scale in the context of simple maps and drawings.
Republic of Ireland	Geography	3rd/4th Class	• Engage in practical use of maps of different scales.
Scotland	Society	Level B/C	• Know about scale on maps.
Wales	Geography	KS 2	• Make maps and plans at a variety of scales.

Landscape gardener

> **Task**
> *You will design your ideal garden from scratch.*

Landscape gardeners spend time planning and designing before any physical work is done in the garden. They need to know the size of plot they are working with and what the owner wants in his/her garden.

1. (a) In a group, decide on the size of your garden, the features you will place in it and the area taken by each feature.

   (b) Design a symbol for the different features in your garden.

   (c) Scale down the area of the garden to draw the plan on A3 $1cm^2$ grid paper.

Overall size of garden (m^2)

Feature	Symbol	Area (m^2)	Scale (cm^2)

2. Draw the scaled plan of the garden and colour appropriately.

3. Show the plan to the rest of the class, explaining your choice of features and their positions.

THINKING MORE ABOUT THINKING
Who did you think about when planning your garden? Were you realistic in your choice of features? Did you allow enough space for each feature? Did you use any specific knowledge when planning your garden?

Teachers notes
Creating

> **The skill of creating involves using previous knowledge to produce new ideas and different ways of seeing things.**

OBJECTIVE:

- Draws and labels an imaginary bird that is perfectly adapted to a particular habitat.

TEACHER INFORMATION:

- The pupils can either use resource material (e.g. encyclopedias, the Internet) for Question 1, or they can use information they may have already studied in lessons about habitats/adaptations.
- There are many adaptive features of birds the pupils may discover. Some are detailed below.

  Bills/beaks: These are adapted to suit feeding habits; for example, a bird's bill may be long and tubular to draw nectar from within a flower; strong and chisel-like to search for insects in the bark of trees; short and hard to break open seed casings; or strong and hooked to tear meat.

  Feet: Birds can have long legs and feet for wading; webbed feet for paddling; sharp talons for grasping prey; agile and nimble feet for grasping tree branches; or strong and short feet to scratch the dirt.

  Wings: These may be adapted to suit gliding at great heights, fast flight, hovering or swimming.

- Before the pupils complete Question 2, they may like to draft their drawings on a separate sheet of paper. Encourage detailed labels; e.g. 'Short, strong beak for eating tough seeds'.

ANSWERS:

Teacher check

ADDITIONAL ACTIVITIES TO DEVELOP THIS SKILL:

- Have the pupils create simple experiments to find out which beak shapes are best for eating different types of food; e.g. using tweezers to pick up seeds etc.
- The pupils can use their drawings to create 3-D clay models of their birds.
- Draw or collect pictures of a variety of animals to make a collage. Label their special features and adaptations.

CURRICULUM LINKS

Country	Subject	Level	Objectives
England	Science	KS 2	• Know how animals in different habitats are suited to their environment.
Northern Ireland	Science	KS 2	• Research topics and investigate habitats.
Republic of Ireland	Science	3rd/4th Class	• Explore ways that animals have adapted to environmental conditions.
Scotland	Science	Level D	• Give examples of how animals are suited to their environment.
Wales	Science	KS 2	• Know how animals in different habitats are suited to their environment.

Superbird!

> ### *Task*
> *You will draw and label a bird that is perfectly adapted to a chosen habitat.*

Birds, like other animals, are adapted to suit their habitat. These adaptations might include the size, shape, texture or the colour of body parts like their beak, feet and wings. They might need these adaptations to keep them warm or cool, to find a mate, to find or eat food or to move about easily.

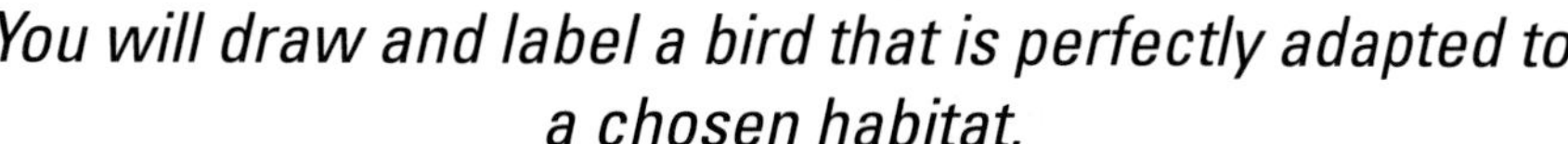

1. Choose one of the habitats below or write your own. Research information about birds that live in that habitat. List some of their characteristics.

Habitat:

☐ *tropical rainforest* ☐ *desert* ☐ *wetland* ☐ *Arctic* ☐ *other* ______________

Bird characteristics:

2. Use your answers to Question 1 to help you draw an imaginary 'superbird' that is perfectly suited to the habitat you chose. Label its special adaptations.

THINKING MORE ABOUT THINKING
What did you think about before you began to draw your bird? Did you 'see' it in your mind's eye? Was it a mixture of different birds you researched or did you completely make it up? How did you decide on which adaptations it should have?

Creating

> The skill of creating involves using previous knowledge to produce new ideas and different ways of seeing things.

OBJECTIVES:

- Completes information about a proposed retail enterprise.
- Designs and draws aspects of a proposed retail enterprise.

TEACHER INFORMATION:

- Pupils will be familiar with shops of various types in the local community either by visiting them or just seeing them.
- Pupils should be familiar with the language relating to retail enterprises, such as 'merchandise', 'clientele', 'advertising', 'suppliers', 'employees' etc.
- All information included, particularly the contact details of suppliers, may be fictitious unless pupils have specific knowledge of suppliers of merchandise and packaging etc.
- Pupils may complete this activity in pairs or small groups as well as individually. They may also wish to share their completed worksheets and drawings and designs with the remainder of the class.

ANSWERS:

Teacher check

ADDITIONAL ACTIVITIES TO DEVELOP THIS SKILL:

- Design and complete an advertising brochure for your new shop.
- Rearrange the information in the boxes on page 91 into a priority order which indicates when each needs to be completed.
- Complete the activity for the same merchandise being sold in a street stall or market.
- Write the advertising text for a newspaper advertisement for your shop.
- Design eye-catching uniforms for the staff of your shop to wear, which may include the shop colours and logo.

CURRICULUM LINKS

Country	Subject	Level	Objectives
England	Geography	KS 2	• Develop decision-making skills and draw plans and maps.
Northern Ireland	Geography	KS 2	• Examine samples from the world around them and use maps.
Republic of Ireland	Geography	3rd/4th Class	• Collect information and make simple maps.
Scotland	Society	Level C	• Record specific information and use maps.
Wales	Geography	KS 2	• Record information and make maps and plans.

A new enterprise

Task
You will formulate a plan for a shop.

THINKING SKILLS • CREATING

1. Complete the shapes by writing the details needed to establish a shop of your own choosing.

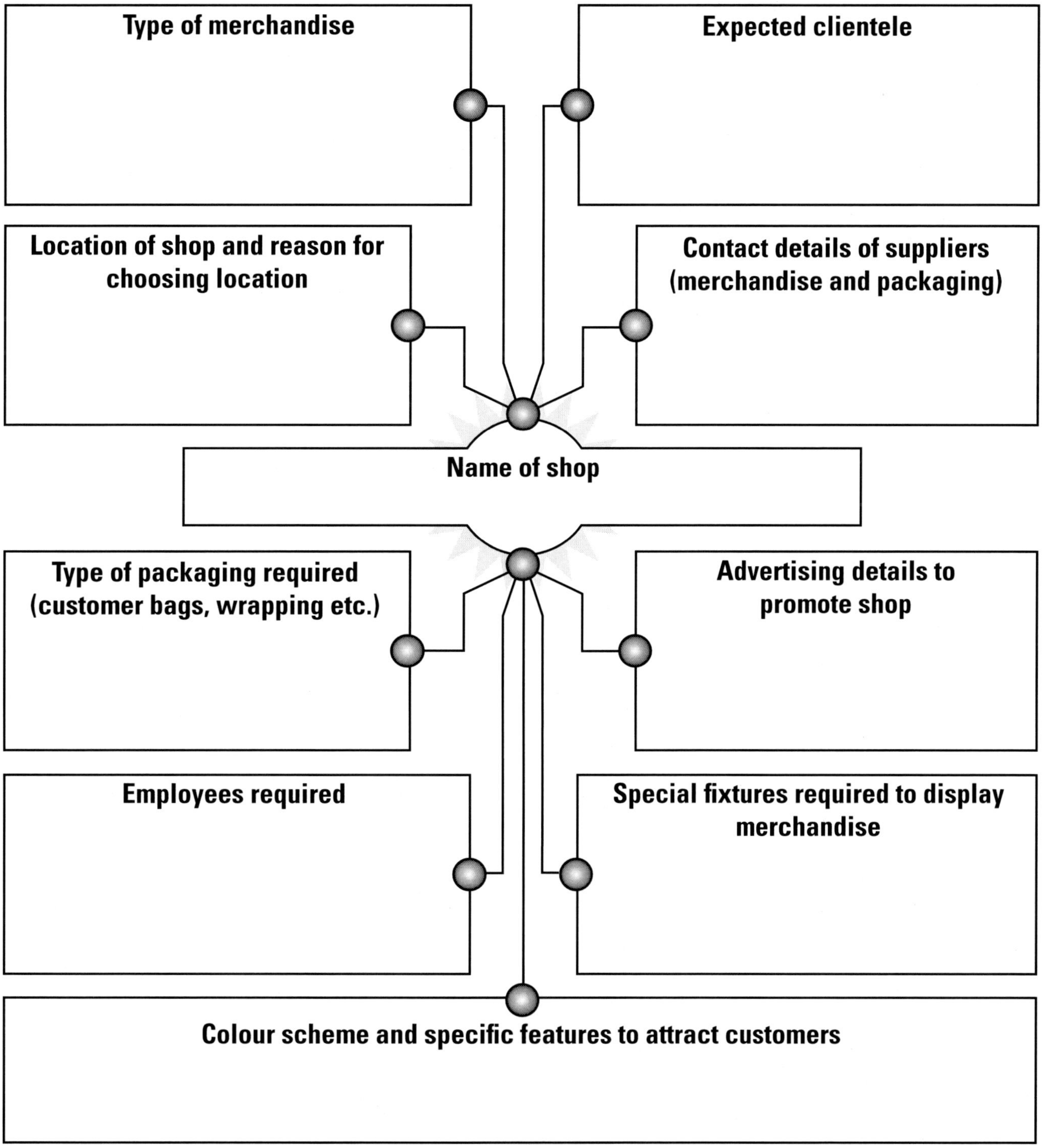
Type of merchandise
Expected clientele
Location of shop and reason for choosing location
Contact details of suppliers (merchandise and packaging)
Name of shop
Type of packaging required (customer bags, wrapping etc.)
Advertising details to promote shop
Employees required
Special fixtures required to display merchandise
Colour scheme and specific features to attract customers

2. On a separate sheet of paper, draw a plan of the layout of your shop, design and draw a shop logo and complete a 3-D drawing, in appropriate colours, of what the interior of your shop will look like when it is ready to open.

THINKING MORE ABOUT THINKING
Were there other details which could have been included, but were not? Do you think that your merchandise and the way it is marketed will be profitable? Why/Why not?

Creating

> The skill of creating involves using previous knowledge to produce new ideas and different ways of seeing things.

OBJECTIVES:

- Devises original track and field events.
- Records equipment required and gives a brief description of each event.

TEACHER INFORMATION:

- Discuss the elements of the traditional track and field events.

  Track: 100 m, 200 m, 400 m, 800 m, 1500 m, 5000 m, 10 000 m, 4 x 100 m relay, 4 x 400 m relay; 110 m, 400 m hurdles, 3000 m steeplechase

  Field: javelin, discus, shot, hammer; long jump, high jump, triple jump, pole vault; heptathlon, decathlon

  Discuss how elements of these events could be incorporated to make new ones. All necessary safety procedures must be adhered to and incorporated into the events.

- Discuss the number of heats that may be required in track events and the number of rounds and attempts in field events.

- Give pupils time to work on the school field with the equipment at their disposal and to test and modify their new events.

ANSWERS:

Teacher check

ADDITIONAL ACTIVITIES TO DEVELOP THIS SKILL:

- Devise a competition schedule for your track and field events. Include the number of entries, heats, rounds etc. Hold a competition to test your schedule.
- Design a poster advertising your competition.
- With a partner, take turns at playing the interviewer and interviewee, of a celebrity athlete who is attending your competition to defend his/her triple gold medal crown.

CURRICULUM LINKS

Country	Subject	Level	Objectives
England	PE	KS 2	• Use running, jumping and throwing skills and take part in and design challenges.
Northern Ireland	PE	KS 2	• Develop core skills of running, jumping and throwing in co-operative and competitive contexts.
Republic of Ireland	PE	3rd/4th Class	• Take part in running, jumping and throwing activities.
Scotland	PE	Level C	• Complete tasks which challenge them to use specific skills.
Wales	PE	KS 2	• Practise skills and follow the rules of an activity.

Track and field

> **Task**
> *You will devise track and field events to be held on your school field.*

Athletes throughout the world take part in track and field events at many different levels, from primary school sports to the Olympics. Since the days of the Ancient Olympic Games, running, throwing and jumping have been part of the athletics tradition.

1. In a group, invent two track and two field events, making full use of the space and equipment available. (You may use well-known events as a guide, but be creative and original.)

name of event	equipment required	brief description
track 1:		
track 2:		
field 1:		
field 2:		

2. Arrange for another group to take part in your track and field events.

THINKING MORE ABOUT THINKING
Have you worked out how to measure and record the results for each person? Have you thought of any problems and planned what to do if they occur? What suggestions could you offer to help people to improve at your events?

Teachers notes

Creating

> **The skill of creating involves using previous knowledge to produce new ideas and different ways of seeing things.**

OBJECTIVES:

- Creates a character from a magazine picture.
- Performs a drama scene using a created character.

TEACHER INFORMATION:

- Teachers will need to provide magazine pictures of people for this activity. The pictures should represent a wide variety of people. Once the pupils have completed the activity, the pictures can be attached to the worksheet.

- Encourage the pupils to create a scene with a clear beginning, middle and end for Question 4. When the majority of the pupils are ready to rehearse their scenes, teachers could time two-minute segments so the pupils get a feel for how long their scenes should take.

- After the pupils have performed for the class, a discussion could be held on how well the characters were portrayed.

ANSWERS:

Teacher check

ADDITIONAL ACTIVITIES TO DEVELOP THIS SKILL:

- Pupils plan and write playscripts or narratives for their created characters.
- Make masks to suit the created characters. Use these in a range of dramatic performances.
- Play a range of creative drama games which involve characterisation.
- Have the pupils imagine what would happen if they met their created character. They could write or role-play their ideas.

CURRICULUM LINKS

Country	Subject	Level	Objectives
England	English	KS 2	• Participate in a wide range of drama activities, including creating different roles and using character to convey story.
Northern Ireland	Language and literacy	KS 2	• Improvise scenes.
Republic of Ireland	English	3rd/4th Class	• Use improvisational drama.
Scotland	Drama	Level C	• Choose and develop a role and work co-operatively with others in role-play.
Wales	English	KS 2	• Participate in a wide range of drama activities, including improvisation and role-play.

Magazine characters

> **Task**
> *You will create a character based on*
> *a magazine picture and plan and perform a scene.*

1. Choose a magazine picture of an interesting person. He/She must be:

   • **someone you do not recognise**   • **someone you would like to role-play.**

2. Create details for your person by completing the facts below. Look carefully at the person's facial expressions, clothes, stance, hair and other features to help you choose suitable answers.

Name ____ Age __________

Lives ____

Family ____

____

Work/Hobbies/Talents ____

____

____

Usual movements (e.g. 'slow, graceful') ____________________________________

____

Voice (e.g. 'loud, rough') ____

Biggest secret ____

____

An animal this person reminds me of: ______________________________________

---

3. Find a partner and discuss the characters you have created.

4. Create a two-minute scene in which your characters meet at a cafe. Why are they meeting? How do they get along? Are they relatives, friends or something else? Discuss these questions and then plan your scene. Divide the action into a beginning, a middle and an end.

5. When you have rehearsed your scene, present it to the class. Introduce your characters before you begin acting.

THINKING MORE ABOUT THINKING
What features gave you the best clues about what your person might be like? What did you think about to 'become' your character? What was the most challenging part of this activity for you? Why?

Thinking challenges 6

Topic focus   **Travel**

Remembering	• On a world map, locate and label the names of the countries you know. • View a segment from a television travel show. When it has finished, list all the facts you can remember.
Understanding	• Choose a city you would like to travel to. Explain why.
Applying	• Write tourist information for your local area, using the style of language found in tourist brochures.
Analysing	• Research to write an article about health tips for travellers. • Plan an adventure holiday to suit a particular age group.
Evaluating	• Suggest improvements that could be made to a tourist attraction you have visited.
Creating	• Create a travel brochure about your favourite holiday destination. • With a partner, write and perform a play about a disastrous holiday.

Topic focus   **That's entertainment!**

Remembering	• List in order the main events of one of your favourite films.
Understanding	• Research to explain what training is required to become a ballet dancer or an opera singer.
Applying	• Find instructions for a simple magic trick. Practise the trick and then perform it for the class.
Analysing	• Write a review for a live performance or film you have seen. • Give your opinion on the following topic: 'It is wrong to make animals perform in a circus'.
Evaluating	• Decide which film, actor and actress you feel deserve Oscars this year. Give reasons.
Creating	• Use materials found in the classroom to make a simple musical instrument. • Every clown has a different design for his/her make-up. Design a clown face that suits your personality.

References

Websites

http://rite.ed.qut.edu.au/oz-teachernet/index.php?module=ContentExpress&func=display&ceid=29

http://www.habits-of-mind.net/whatare.htm

http://www.edhelper.com

http://ictnz.com/articles/quallearn.html

http://www.gse.buffalo.edu/fas/shuell/CEP564/Metacog.htm

http://chiron.valdosta.edu/whuitt/col/cogsys/bloom.html

http://coe.sdsu.edu/eet/Articles/bloomrev/index.htm

http://www.learningandteaching.info/learning/bloomtax.htm

www.enchantedlearning.com/graphicorganizers/

http://www.graphic.org/goindex.html

www.edwdebono.com/

http://www.kaganonline.com/AboutKaganFrame.html

http://www.kurwongbss.eq.edu.au/thinking/Think%20Keys/keys.htm

http://www.infed.org/thinkers/gardner.htm

Books

Habits of Mind: A Developmental Series by Arthur L. Costa and Bena Kallick